STOP
WAITING
FOR PRINCE
CHARMING!

He's Already Married to Bob.

The Odds of Getting Married
and Other Nonsense

Anita Reinsma

ISBN: 0615476899
ISBN-13: 9780615476896

Names, identifying characteristics
and locations have been changed.

Dedicated with love to Rich Tanzmann,
Don Herbert and my daughter, Christina.

$\mathcal{I}$NTRODUCTION

Stop waiting for Prince Charming! He's already married to Bob. I know this sounds crazy, but it's true. Then again, the Prince Charming of our title (now happily married to Bob) wasn't meant for you anyway. Your problem was and maybe still is that you are WAITING for Prince Charming. Because you are a patient person, *you do waiting well.* Yes, I said, "You do *waiting well.*"

The idea of waiting for Prince Charming is hideous propaganda. The only time you should be waiting for anything is at the bakery, and that's for fresh croissants.

You've probably watched the talk shows on finding the "right" guy. You've probably read the books. *Both are useless.* Disregard their advice completely. This book is in your hands to guide you to *unique and different techniques* for finding him … or for him to discover you.

Life has gotten impersonal, complicated, confusing, frustrating and demoralizing. The wonderful part of this is that you can be in charge. You really can make it your own joyful circus. Life is crazy so you need to live it that way. Go for something a bit more insane. *Insane is good.*

Finally, as an extraordinary bonus, I've included some recipes in this book. I just figured it was a thoughtful gesture. Seeing how everyone is addicted to cooking shows and desperate for the newest concoction. I swear, it could be a cheese puff casserole with chopped celery, and it would be featured on *Good Morning America.*

The recipes within these pages are not my own creations. I am a bad cook. Make my *original* recipes, and you could be risking your life. I don't want the liability.

CONTENTS

"Always be sincere, even if you don't mean it."
~ Harry S. Truman, U.S. President

Scary statistic: A woman over age 40 has a better chance of being killed by a terrorist than of getting married.

Exercise, Playing Games, Swimming, Bicycling, Skiing. Yodeling, Camping: Noun or Verb?, Exotic Lands & Tours, Kayaking, Speed-Dating, The Internet, Social Networking, Blind Date

The Obvious, Gym, Supermarkets and Warehouse Stores, Home Improvement Stores, Parties, Alaska, A

"Silly is you in a natural state and serious is something you have to do until you can get silly again."
~Mike Myers, Actor

$\mathcal{A}$CKNOWLEDGING THE SILLY HEARTS:

Thank you, David Letterman, Paul Shaffer, Roseanne Barr, Joy Behar, Mark & Brian, Connie Mueller, Richard Allen, Patty Reinsma, Kathleen Fernan, Debbie Andersen, Conan, Jimmy Fallon, Chelsea Handler, Craig Ferguson, John Lithgow…just to name a few!

ODDS OF GETTING MARRIED

There I was lying face down on the floor in my neighborhood bank when I thought about a statistic I once heard. I don't, as a habit, lie face down on the floor in my bank, but the robbers insisted on it.

The puzzling statistic, *"A woman over age 40 has a better chance of being killed by a terrorist than of getting married,"* has been widely circulated. With my logic, I put the robbers into the same category as terrorists. So, in the grand scheme of things, I concluded that my odds now were better than ever for getting remarried at any age! As long as I didn't get shot first, that is.

Entering the bank that fateful day, I walked through the door and came face-to-face with a masked gunman with a huge automatic weapon. I stopped immediately. We stared at each other for a quick moment, and then with the barrel of his gun, he motioned for me to go further inside and get down on the floor. Not one to argue with a lethal weapon of any kind, I did as suggested.

1

What immediately went through my mind was what I happened to be wearing. I had on a hideous Hawaiian shirt that could glow in the dark. The last thing you want in a situation like this is to be noticed. You want to blend in and be invisible.

I remained motionless on the floor wondering how this robbery would play out. Grab and run? Shots being fired? What about the news cameras and reporters coming to the scene afterwards? Video puts 10 pounds on you! I would look like a big fatso.

How is my hair? Are my roots showing? I started to feel moist. I was nervous. I needed to calm down. *Don't move. Don't make eye contact,* I told myself. Would I sweat and rub off my eyebrows while lying here? No, what would be even worse, I could be taken as the hostage. A scenario presented itself in my head: The leader shouts, "Hey, lady, you, with the hideous shirt, you're coming with us."

By now, an imprint of the carpet pattern had been pressed into my face. I haven't seen that look featured in *Glamour* magazine lately. The bank employees would describe me as a short, middle-aged woman, a Berber carpet imprint on her cheek, half an eyebrow and wearing a hideous Hawaiian shirt. The security camera footage would be released. I imagined Stacy London of the TV show *What Not to Wear* shrieking, "Look at that shirt! Talk about what not to wear!"

Don't forget that this was happening in Southern California, where breaking news can be a car chase. News helicopters would be hovering and following our every move. All regular television programming would be interrupted. Second by second, the chase would be covered. Wild speculation would take place as to whether I, the "hostage," am actually part of the heist! Was I an accomplice? The news media would descend upon my neighbors. My friends would be hounded incessantly for more details. Were they aware of my life of crime?

The robbers/kidnappers would force me into the car, then we'd race through the city to make our getaway. I'd explain to the leader that kidnapping is a far more serious crime than robbery. I would recite lengthy jail sentences they might face to convince them that I, simply put, was not worth the trouble. Could Dog the Bounty Hunter be far behind?

The leader, now realizing that I'd make their lives miserable because I hadn't shut up, would order his assistant to push me out of the car.

"Dump her!"

I'd tumble from the vehicle. Police and paparazzi would come to a screeching halt. Thank God none of that ever happened! Back to the bank …

After what seemed to be an hour, actually five minutes, a bank employee announced that the team of robbers had left. The police arrived and began their investigation. I mentioned to Officer Jensen (I picked him to chat with because he didn't have a wedding ring on) that when I entered the bank and saw the robbers, I thought about turning and running. Since the lead robber had a huge automatic weapon, I froze right there in the doorway. When the robber motioned me into the bank, I complied because I figured within seconds I could be felled by a hail of bullets.

Officer Jensen said with authority, "The bad guys with those weapons rarely know how to use them. In fact, most don't know how to aim. You probably would have been fine if you would have turned and ran."

I told him I would keep that in mind for the next time I walked into a bank and came face-to-face with an automatic weapon.

He asked if I recalled the voice or voices of the robbers. Did they have an accent or anything unusual in their speech pattern? I explained to him that I heard very little. While lying down on the carpet, I had my left ear, the good ear, against the ground. My right ear hears nothing. It is completely deaf. I continued to explain, "That right ear is really only there for decorative purposes."

Officer Jensen quickly dismissed me as a worthless witness. He remained all business during this investigation and obviously wasn't concerned about getting to know me or the fact that I happened to be available Thursday night.

I exited the bank realizing that it was essential to repair my psyche as well as my eyebrow. This was a harrowing, life-changing experience. I immediately drove to the mall for some retail therapy and chocolate.

(This essay has been reenacted on *You Tube.*)

TALENTS, ADVENTURES AND TECHNIQUES

EXERCISE

Get out there and partner up with someone for some exercise. I do a lot of different things with Rich. He's an artist, a silly heart and just a touch goofy so we have a fantastic time together. At some point in our lively association, he and I agreed that it was time to begin an exercise routine. It was important that we do it together because we knew each other too well. I would say, "I jogged," and I would not have. He would say he jogged, and he would not have. We basically knew each other to be liars. Let's not overlook the fact that it was summertime. I saw this as another crucial research project with the mission of locating good-looking, datable guys. An added bonus was that that they would be wearing skimpy clothing as they jogged around the track. *I have no shame.*

We decided to start sometime within the next week. It would be good for us and therapeutic. This decision also dictated the urgent need to shop as we needed appropriate jogging attire. We accompanied one another to the mall, both realizing our goal of looking nice on the track. We both approved of our respective selections. The other joggers would probably gasp as we raced passed them. We looked that good!

The following week, we arrived at the high-school track looking, dare I say, breathtaking. Spot-on Nike users. We calculated what we needed to accomplish that evening and began the jog. Ten minutes into our run, I was slowing down. So Rich fell back to stay beside me. Fifteen minutes into our jog, we were practically down to a walk. He could see that I was sweating. He was showing signs of moisture as well.

I said, "We are sweating. We're going to ruin our outfits." This was unacceptable. We sat down for a moment. We had not factored in sweating as part of this activity. We both had made major investments in these pants, t-shirts, the jackets we had tied fashionably around our waists, the shoes and socks, the sweat bands at the wrist and on the forehead. When we had stepped onto the track, we'd both looked fabulous. *Now?* Our hair was matted from the sweat. My makeup was beginning to look like Alice Cooper's. Evidence of a sweaty workout was prominently displayed on our designer jogging suits. We were bordering on a public display of tackiness. The fashion police wouldn't even want to frisk us.

We left the track determined to re-evaluate our effort and find a more enjoyable way to challenge ourselves. A perfect place for reflection is Baskin-Robbins. After a hot fudge sundae, we had an epiphany! We will join a chess club!

PLAYING GAMES

What is playing games anyway? You might say that it's smart people sitting around tables with all manner of game boards making moves. Or they could be sitting around tables playing cards. The important thing here is that there is no sweating involved.

Of course, Rich and I would require a wardrobe appropriate for the occasion. Something they would wear in the Hamptons. Classy, washable silk would be lovely. This decision about playing chess also coincided with our continuing goal to make friends and influence people without spending too much on gas money. We were going to play chess at the local university, namely Caltech, which was two miles away.

Maybe we didn't think the clothing thing out properly since the other players — students — were in jeans and decades-old t-shirts. Rules were posted by the sign-in sheet. No talking during play. The room was to be quiet. No hooting or disparaging remarks such as your opponent is stupid! (The people at CalTech have IQs of

731. No one is stupid there!) For the most part, the only words to be spoken were "Check" and "Checkmate." Actually, we were both grateful that the students wouldn't be striking up conversations. We knew nothing about quantum physics or the time and space continuum. I could carry on a lively conversation about Sponge Bob Square Pants. That's about it.

To our opponents, we were mediocre chess players with nice clothes. That was fine. We needed to experience a new activity, new people, and that is what we were doing. Actually, it turned out to be a bit boring. Cooped up inside, no shrieking and celebrating when anyone got to "Checkmate." *C'mon.*

On the way home, we decided that lawn bowling could be fun. It's outside. There are friendly people. Most are older and retired but one or two of the men could be *available.* They are vocal about their jubilation when the game goes well. Granted some would need to be cautious about jumping around too much. They could break a hip.

We went to Rich's house to register for the Arcadia Lawn Bowling Club which meets twice a week! We read the rules. They required players to wear traditional, all white attire. We were ecstatic! Right here in print. They were insisting we purchase a special wardrobe! Crisp cotton, scuff-free white shoes, and we were on our way. When we arrived at the bowling green, we both looked marvelous!

We lasted for a month and realized that the leisurely pace was more than we could tolerate. *Throw the ball. Watch it roll. Snore.* We needed more of a challenge! I suggested the NASCAR racing school. Don't overlook that this would require some really outrageous clothes!

SWIMMING

Swimming is a fabulous way to work out. In Southern California, you can swim year-round. There are private and public pools galore. Go to Vegas, and you'll find pools are the places to party. How could you not find a body beautiful at this martini-laden Nevada reservoir? Meanwhile, I am reluctant to put my chubby body into a bathing suit. But the solution occurred to me while watching Michael Phelps. He wears a wonderful, long, black body-suit, and it could work nicely for me. It's total coverage from neck to ankle!

We have very few swimmable lakes in the Los Angeles area. Toluca Lake, Westlake, Lake Forest are all pretend lakes. They're private and gated communities. No one is allowed to swim in those lakes. There are even cities with "lake" in their names. They might sound bucolic, inviting and be in close proximity to where you live! But don't be too quick about packing your bathing suit, fins and snorkel. There's usually not so much as a body of water even in or near those cities!

The Pacific Ocean is a great place for lots of recreational activities. Plenty of good looking, athletic men and women keep us safe on the beaches. Lifeguards have a job to do because the ocean is a dangerous place.

I love those couples who enjoy long, romantic walks on the beach. They stroll hand-in-hand chatting as the ocean waves lap at their feet. Have *you* ever walked in the sand? *It is hard. It is exhausting.*

If you walk where the surf comes in, the sand is wet. Your feet will sink down as the water swirls around, and you have to kind of push off for the next step. If the sand is dry, you still have to exert a lot of effort to get one foot in front of the other. My experience in trying to traverse the sand is one of abject failure. I get about 20 feet into my journey, and I'm huffing and puffing. My face is bright red. I begin waving at the lifeguards to bring the defibrillator before I do a face plant. How can anyone have a conversation while walking in the sand?

As for swimming in the ocean, I don't. Be forewarned, there are inherent risks. I will go to the beach, watch the surfers, and collect sea shells. All benign activities. But swimming in the ocean is not a recreational sport. There are special terms for something that will kill you in an instant. *Undertow. Riptide.* These two words mean terror. Sheer terror. Enter the ocean, and you could be a goner. This is a current that will scoop you up, then carry you away from the shoreline and life as you have known it. You will need the services of the lifeguard to rescue you … unless he doesn't see you because he is talking to a Pamela Anderson look-alike over at Tower 10.

The ocean is home to creatures with teeth. Some creatures have stingers, hence the term "sting ray." If you're near a reef, you could encounter moray eels. They live in little crevices, caves and on ledges. Eels have powerful jaws. When they launch themselves at you, it's not because they're hungry. No, my friend. You are an unwelcome visitor.

Most creatures in the ocean hate us. Is that so hard to comprehend? We are invading the sanctity of their home. They have to retaliate. They can deliver pain. If they are really pissed off, they will eat us.

BICYCLING

Bicycling was a chance for my good friend, Rich, and me to enjoy an activity together and meet new people. But neither one of us rides like Lance Armstrong. We fall off our bikes if we look around too much. You could call it a balance disorder, I suppose. We both lament that our bicycling skills are marginal. Equilibrium eludes us.

We were reluctant to venture onto bike trails with too many other riders. We sought out the deserted ones. So we never met anyone. The park was pleasant but not a hotbed for social networking. As time wore on, neither one of us had gotten the proper techniques down yet. If there's a sharp curve in the bike path, we've been seen swerving and crashing into bushes. We would have to plan our routes according to how much vegetation lined the path so we could avoid serious injury or, truth to told, DEATH if we careened into the great unknown.

The whole biking thing did not last long for me. After a month, my balance still wasn't improving. Going around corners was my biggest problem. Speed also felt tricky. My brain would go stupid on me, and I would begin braking too late. As a result, twice (yes, that would be two times) I slid the bike sideways, flipped it over and found myself underneath a parked car. After the second time, I gave my bike to Goodwill.

If your boyfriend insists on a bike ride, get a built-for-two model. Sit behind him. It's tricky for the person in front to check whether the person in back is doing anything at all — like peddling! The idea is not to! Since you only need one hand on the handle bars, your other hand is free to hold a refreshing beverage (read: Martini) while you enjoy the scenery.

One of the most pleasant experiences you could have is a bike trip through Switzerland. There is a special tour that takes just over a week with nightly stops in villages along the way. It's at a leisurely pace so you get to know your fellow bikers and spend time visiting with your hosts. It is a beautiful immersion into the countryside and the fine citizens of the country! It's usually scheduled for the late spring so the meadows would be lush with wildflowers. The cattle will be snacking in the tall grass, and we could be entertained by the cow bells clanging throughout the valley.

I would feel confident in my riding skills since we would be scooting along the open Swiss countryside at about 5 miles per hour. That's not even fast enough for bugs to get stuck to your teeth! We would be on country roads so if I fell over with my bike, there would be little chance that I could be run over by a car. A herd of goats, *maybe.*

I signed up for this adventure when I discovered that you actually coast the whole way down the route! The first village is at the highest elevation so peddling is hardly necessary! The guides swear that you will not experience even the remotest level of exhaustion on this bike ride. It's all quite civilized because you arrive at each town checking into the bed and breakfast at about five in the afternoon or as some refer to it "wine o'clock." Excellent scheduling as far as I am concerned!

On the second day several miles into our afternoon leg, a torrential rain storm swept down on us. That's when I remembered why I hated the outdoors and, for the most part, had avoided it.

SKIING

A few winters back I was invited to go snow skiing with some co-workers. The outing wasn't going to be for three weeks so I had a chance to practice a little. Southern California isn't known as a Mecca for winter sports. To experience a true alpine adventure, we go to Disneyland to ride the Matterhorn bobsleds. Our mountains at the higher elevations get snow annually but it's usually just a slight dusting. So when the conditions are right and snow lands on our ski slopes, sticks to the ground and becomes a measureable amount, the snowfall itself becomes a huge news story worldwide!

Satellite trucks race up the mountains. Cameras just inches away from the snow pull back to reveal majestic peaks of white. Reporters explain the phenomenon of rain becoming snow for the stupid among us. If it has snowed a few feet, instead of inches, people go crazy! Everyone is wildly excited. Most of the time, the snow doesn't last long. In fact, you usually have to scurry up there to experience it, touch it, and play in it because by mid-afternoon the snow has melted.

This particular winter was a gift. Those of us in Southern California were bundled up in coats and scarves because it was getting down to 40 degrees at night. Several storms brought 20 feet of snow to the mountains so we were looking at a situation not unlike the Swiss Alps! The resort spokespeople were giddy.

They were reporting the conditions: *packed snow, powder snow, depth.* This was heaven!

While up north visiting my brother in the land of the freezing cold, I did do some cross-country skiing. Cross-country skiing, incidentally, is the best way to kill someone. Take a person, like me, who is out of shape. Put them in 25 pounds of arctic clothing, strap on a backpack weighing 15 pounds with survival food, put 20-foot long skis on their feet, and start walking/skiing across the frozen land. I don't care that the ground is flat. I couldn't get anywhere. While it seemed like I had been making no progress, it felt as if I was exerting unbelievable effort. I had to lean forward, then push and slide my skis through 3 feet of soft snow. The ideal way to do this is to develop a rhythm. After about 10 minutes, not even my heart had a rhythm. I made it less than a third of a mile. I collapsed. I saw my life pass before my eyes. Some sports are not worth near death experiences!

Anyway, back to my upcoming ski adventure. I was concerned that I hadn't been skiing for several years. I figured the best thing that I could do was practice ahead of time. I would drive up to the slopes, rent some equipment, and go for a few runs. My date wasn't for two more weekends so that gave me plenty of time to perfect my slalom skills.

As my history dictates, I had to purchase a ski outfit, gloves and a hat before I could move forward with anything else. I am completely aware that I could rent the sportswear. However, doing that creeps me out. Where has the clothing been? Who wore it? Did the last person who wore the clothes meet an untimely death by skiing off a cliff? The karma is too iffy. Of course, I was justifiably fearful of the expense of purchasing something brand new. I hoped refinancing the condo wouldn't be necessary. Luckily, I found pants and a jacket which were constructed with a slick, shiny fabric. Both were on sale. I was a fashion statement. After that, boots, skis and poles could be rented up the mountain.

Driving up into the winter wonderland was exciting. I kept thinking about the talent in the Olympics — free style skiing, slaloming, flying over moguls. My expertise is the bunny slope but that day I planned to try the main run. I figured visualization would be a good idea. I imagined myself as a championship skier. I parked my car, opened the door, and stepped outside. The air was cold and crisp. This was to be a perfect day for me! *"The thrill of victory. The agony of defeat!"* I took a deep breath, and with my second step, I slipped on the snow and landed on my butt.

I walked over to the rental area to pick up my equipment. The young man asked what level of skier I was. I didn't want to look stupid so I replied, "Moderate." My hope was that he wouldn't look out the window and see me doing uncontrolled cartwheels down the ski run. A bad skier is one thing. A habitual liar is another!

I exited the lodge ready for an adventurous afternoon. Near the lift, I found a bench where I could buckle on the boots and skis. I gripped the poles, and I stood up. I unsteadily walked/skied over to the lift. I grabbed the side bar of the chair as it swung around, and I jumped on. The wind was in my face. What a great feeling!

Within seconds, I was 60 feet above the ground. I recognized that I had a lengthy ascent before I would be unceremoniously dumped off at the end of the lift. So I relaxed and enjoyed the view. During this peaceful time, we were going higher and higher and higher! Soon I was asking myself some startling questions ...

Why didn't I practice a little before jumping on this contraption?

Why didn't I check the map to identify the easier runs?

How was I going to get off the lift without killing myself? It had been years since I skied! What was I thinking?

My next question was: *Will the ski lift ever stop?* I swear I can see the curvature of the earth! I now hung thousands of feet in the air. I thought, *I am in the LA to New York flight path. Look over there, that's an American Airlines jet* ...the flight attendant handed a Diet Coke to the guy in the window seat.

Finally, the lift was coming up to the top and starting its return swing around. It was ready to pitch me off. I was trying to scan the markers for the less treacherous runs. All I could see were black diamonds everywhere. There wasn't a smiley face among them!

The lift jerked forward. I flew 5 feet into the air. I landed on my skis, and I was immediately on a swift descent that I believe broke the land-speed record. I barreled downhill, totally out of control. The main objective going through my mind was to stop further acceleration. I should sit down. *I did.*

The fashionable outfit I bought had been on sale. It was a nice jumpsuit but not perfect for skiing per se. That "per se" is important. The fabric is a nonstick nylon. When I sat down, I didn't stick to the snow. Instead, the fabric actually allowed me to pick up speed while descending! The only way to stop this madness would be for the ski patrol to throw out a spiked speed strip.

I careened past other skiers while still sitting on my butt. It occurred to me that if I leaned way over to my side and dug my hands into the snow, I might be able to stop. Either I try this maneuver or I'd be looking forward to years of plastic surgery after my face smacked into a tree. I tilted way over to my right, and with a sideways motion dug into the snow. Finally I came to a halt! I breathed a sigh of relief. Within seconds, a good-looking man approached me to ask if I was OK.

I looked up at him. It was as if I couldn't remember what language I spoke. I was relieved and felt comforted when he asked if he could help me. He didn't just walk me over to the lift. William rode it with me and skied down the run three times right by my side! My confidence was rebuilt.

When he excused himself to join his *boyfriend* in the lodge, I wanted to throw myself off a cliff. But hold on there, gentle reader! He invited me to go with him to the Lodge. He offered to pair me up with another skier for the rest of the afternoon.

I went with him!

He smiled and said, "I have some friends here who would love to hang out with you. They're on the United States Olympic Ski Team. I'll set you up with them!"

His words reverberated in my head–United States Olympic Ski Team.

We entered the Lodge and snaked our way over to a large group of young men and women. They were all happy to see him and were very welcoming to me. As he introduced us, I was carefully examining each one of these guys. Who would he be passing me off to–Jake, Terrence, Roger, Adam or Johnny?

William was saving the best for last. He smiled broadly and rather dramatically gestured over to his right, "And here are my friends who are members of the United States Olympic Ski Team.

"Anita, I would like you to meet Tracy, Kimberly and Chloe."

YODELING

It is underrated. You can practice yodeling in the car while you're alone. Then impress your new boyfriend and friends when you can sound like someone straight out of the Alps! They even have "how to yodel CDs" on Amazon or down the street at Best Buy if you're really serious.

Bear in mind that special talents can be brought into your life by someone you meet and would like to get to know better. He could be a championship yodeler. The original "Yahoooo" was a yodel!

Distinctive and unique talents are to be enjoyed. If he does bird calls all day long, you could have a nervous breakdown after a week. Be careful with this one!

CAMPING. NOUN OR VERB?

Camping is one of those activities you either like or just plain hate. This concept of camping is an important issue. Notice I said *issue.* I did not say *adventure, event, outing, escape.* I don't "get" camping whether it is a noun or a verb. I will have neither in my vocabulary.

Friends invited me to go camping. They thought I might enjoy it. Meanwhile, the great outdoors for me is poolside in a cabana, palm trees swaying, the fragrance of the Plumeria flower floating through the air while I relax on a chaise lounge, and, oh look, I am one sip away from ordering another Pina Colada.

My introduction to this camping adventure *du jour* was to spend four hours bouncing around in a truck while traversing dirt roads though the Southern California desert. Through the haze of the setting sun, we spotted the campsite on the barren horizon. I was convinced that this was a part of our world that Google had yet to discover! There was a circle of tents with trucks, cars and dirt bikes off to the side. A robust bonfire presented a welcoming glow. Did they have coffee brewing? How about some scones to go with it?

Food. Pack sensible things that you will eat whether heated or cold. People have been known to survive on Fritos for entire camping weekends. I was with serious campophiles. They had brought the ingredients for breakfast — eggs, bacon, hash browns and sausage with pan-fried breads. *Stop right there.* I forgot the mention of corned beef hash! Now, that's something you eat at a diner in Shreveport, Louisiana. This was the California desert. How do you properly wash up the pans, plates and utensils (let alone your hands) after this grease-packed meal?

I vote for those little Variety Pack cereal boxes that you peel open. The box itself is used as a bowl, the milk is poured in, and you're ready to eat. That's a simple, hearty meal and no cleanup is required.

Everyone was responsible for their own food and preparation. I was fortunate that my friends told me they had everything under control. I needn't do anything. Had it been left to me I would've towed a satellite dish behind the car so I could have called out for deliveries whether they were by land or by air with helicopter drops.

The primitive accommodation of restroom facilities bears a mention but it almost brings me to tears. For heaven's sake, would it be that much of an imposition to install a mirror in the restroom? Instead, there was a large stainless steel type cookie sheet that was supposed to serve as a reflective surface. I think it was salvaged from a fun house. It's more evidence that a guy, who routinely pees behind a tree, selected this particular spot without considering any of the females.

For the daytime activity, most went off to ride their dirt bikes. As each person rode off, a cloud of dust enveloped our encampment. I blinked the dirt out of my eyes just in time to see them disappear behind the dunes.

I was left to entertain myself. However I had been warned: *Don't go hiking because of rattle snakes. And don't swim in the lake because it's polluted.* Truth be told, it was the kind of a lake found in horror movies. The water was murky, which led me to imagine dead bodies were inches below the surface. I decided to park myself in a lawn chair and read a book.

As I sat there alone, I wondered where the coyotes were. *Napping?* You know, that desert area is populated with all manner of vicious beasts — coyotes, bobcats, hyenas, wild boars. Of course, I was guessing. But in the quiet of the afternoon, I imagined all of these blood-thirsty animals sitting inside the bushes conspiring together. I assumed that they had gotten the memo about the lake water being contaminated so they were looking for a drink — water, blood, Diet Coke, who knew? I covered our stack of bottled water as a precaution.

A few hours later, the little army of adventurers appeared on the horizon. As they approached, I could see they were covered in dirt. That's what this is all about — dirt bike riding. I could hear them shouting, "We need food!" Were they talking to me? I turned around to see if someone else had walked up behind me. Someone like Wolfgang Puck. Was he here somewhere? I certainly was not the person they needed if they were faint from hunger.

Strangers have expectations. It was dinnertime. They were returning to camp and felt hungry. I knew nothing about what anyone brought to eat or wanted to eat. All I know when it comes to camping food is the long-treasured traditional recipe for S'mores. *That's it.* (Graham crackers, Hershey semi-sweet chocolate candy bar, large marshmallows. Put the marshmallow on a wire coat hanger that has been pulled apart to serve as a long metal rod, extend it above the open flame of bonfire, toast marshmallow until brown and melting. Make a graham cracker sandwich with chocolate bar and melting marshmallow. Enjoy.)

Well, as fate would have it, my friends had decided on burgers for this feast. There was a six-inch hibachi which would be used to cook the burgers. The size of the hibachi meant one burger, maybe two, would cook simultaneously. We would have this crowd fed by next month according to my calculations. Then, to myself, I questioned how safe this meat was. Had it been refrigerated? Had it been kept under blocks of ice? Were they able to properly wash their hands to make the burger patties? Did we have condiments? I can't eat a burger without crispy lettuce.

This deprivation and overall agony would last for several more days. I made the commitment and would see it through. Since there was no bus stop in sight, I had no choice. I did make the best of it. My friends were subjecting me to cruel and unusual punishment. They reminded me that, if anything, I could write about this weekend. Sure, if I lived through it, that is.

I have to admit that I was thoroughly entertained by the mosquitoes as they swooped in to suck the blood from my body. I had so much pest repellant on that I was probably affecting insects in the six surrounding counties! The mosquitoes were smart. As they were about to land on me, they would hover. I was practically eye-to-eye, nose-to-nose with them. I was certain that I heard them cursing as they were forced into reverse upon smelling my bug-be-dead spray and repellants. In this small way, I conquered the wild. I was happy and proud.

The last night, a slight cool breeze kicked up. It was really fabulous. A perfect evening which seemed to make all things right. Life was good. It was my reward for suffering through days without a shower and a flush toilet.

Actually, the slight breeze was the payoff for all of us. We had immersed ourselves in nature, and we were being rewarded. However, the cooling breeze brought with it thousands, no, hundreds of thousands, of teeny-tiny spiders that we didn't detect until the morning. Some of us had hundreds of bites or hundreds of thousands of bites! I had little red welts from head to toe. I felt miserable.

As everyone was packing up, I overheard plans for more campouts. *Kill me now!*

It was years after this camping trip when something extremely important came to my attention. For quite some time, I and many others who were going to be in and around Bugland sprayed ourselves with repellant. After a decade of research, it was documented that lab rats, when sprayed with repellant, became confused, and they also developed brain tumors and severe physical problems.

Their conclusion: *Bug-be-dead sprays and repellants should NEVER be applied directly onto the skin.* I did plenty of that over the years. Considering the *amount* of those chemicals I have doused onto my body, I will either be carted off to a mental hospital or a third eye will grow in middle of my forehead.

Bottom line? If someone asks you to go camping, my advice is: *Just say no.*

EXOTIC LANDS & TOURS

Tours are a great way to get out into the world. I'm not talking about the Giddy Up Gambling Getaway Bus to Vegas. I am suggesting that you put your feet onto another continent. Have a totally unique experience! Many people book a rail trip through Europe. Consider another continent and explore Africa instead. Go on a safari. Be among the privileged to see gorillas in their natural habitat. Besides enjoying the extraordinary beauty of the African continent, you'll find that the safari guides are stunning. They are a completely different breed of the male species. They are take-your-breath-away good looking.

Accommodations can range from a tent to a magnificent lodge. They're always located in the middle of the action. Be cautious about the Serengeti Migration because you don't want 10,000 wildebeest trampling you to death during the middle of the night because you pitched your tent in the wrong place! I can promise you that with some lodges, right at sunrise, you can stand on your deck and safely observe lions, elephants and rhinos at the nearby waterhole. That early morning scenery is nicer than looking at the driveup menu to order morning coffee and an Egg McMuffin!

There's absolutely no question that traveling outside the United States has its risks. All of these countries and continents have been beautifully represented by the Discovery Channel. What the documentaries don't expose you to is the dark side! You need to prepare yourself for the food, customs, and for the walking. Special documentation and visas may be required. You will need a series of shots to avoid getting malaria and other diseases.

Recently, a woman returned from Uganda only to be hospitalized for weeks. However, it took a year for the doctors to diagnose her problem. She had contracted a viral disease much like Ebola. Her itinerary included a visit to the Queen Elizabeth National Park. Inside the park is a cave with hundreds of thousands of bats. I don't know about you but I cannot imagine why that cave would be fascinating to see. In addition to all of the bats were all of their droppings. The latter was the source of the lethal disease. I'm sure she had one of those multiple choice itineraries:

- Visit a dark, dank cave full of bat poop.
- Go to the Mumdada Mall.
- Weave a straw hat with the friendly women of the nearby village.

Go figure!

The Amazon Rainforest in South America can provide a setting for another fantastic adventure. It looks like an expansive green world of vegetation with exotic creatures everywhere. Television makes it look accessible so you feel capable of visiting this lush jungle. It may cover thousands of acres but other tourists have done it. *Why not you?*

No one even knows how many species of animals and insects are in the Amazon region. This means that they don't know how many poisonous ones there are either — animals or insects. That's tempting fate. This is the reality of exploration.

You are at one with nature. You're perched on a seat in a dugout canoe floating down the Amazon River. You can hear the birds in the triple canopy above, and see monkeys playfully swinging through the trees. This is a pretty picture. It's exhilarating. However, when you glance down into the water, you'll see two-foot-long, people-eating piranhas trying to chew up the wooden oars on either side of the canoe. If the canoe is a wooden hull vessel, they'll snack on that next. Poisonous snakes are swarming nearby. They're waiting for the canoe to capsize.

But there is more to the Amazon River adventure, and it seems incomprehensible! The knowledgeable experts (an oxymoron) who conduct the tours discuss with great authority the *mood* of the river and its *temper*. "Watch out. The Amazon is crabby today." Yep, that's exactly what you want to hear as you're approaching the rapids around that next curve!

Please, don't get me started on all of the weird vegetation that thrives in this humid environment. These plants are extraordinarily beautiful, delicate, nothing like you have ever seen before. Only botanical experts can identify the magical medicinal plants so you can't just start chewing on fruit from the nearby shrubbery thinking it will cure your athlete's foot. With more than 40,000 species (That's a guess. Not an accurate count), you have to be extremely careful. Some plants have a sap which is used for poison darts. Get a scratch on your thigh from that bad boy, and you'll be returning home in a pine box.

There are no sidewalks. You're traipsing through a jungle. Always watch where you're walking. Snapping turtles can amputate your toes. "Invisible" insects are prolific. You could casually lean against a guava tree and within five seconds bizarre parasites are crawling all over you. They will eat you alive. Oh, yeah, I forgot about the several hundred species of intestinal vermin that thrive here, too!

While on the subject of travel, I could not overlook a mistake made by many beginners. I hope you will steer clear of this blunder. The exotic, the mysterious, and the magic should be on the "to do" list. But it's the weather patterns that must be considered first and foremost when an excursion is in the works. Summer here. Winter there. Different hemispheres. Be realistic. What's within walking distance of your hotel? Is it the equator or the North Pole?

I have witnessed neophytes making plans for singles cruises and tours to outrageous places. Each time, without exception, they were persuaded to book because of the price. One excursion was to the Scandinavian countries with visits to quaint villages and rides via horse drawn carriage. All this old world charm plus reasonable airfare and nice accommodations for an itty bitty amount of money! Pinch me! Really? There has to be a catch.

The catch was the departure date. It was in the dead of winter. It gets freezing cold there in that part of the world. Why would anyone go to the Baltic Sea in winter? The only reason I could imagine is that you've taken a job on a fishing trawler because you've run out of employment options here at home.

This was an itinerary that needed to be scrutinized. What is the average temperature in Stockholm in December? Is it below zero or *way* below zero? Will any extensive land travel be accomplished by dog sled? While on the ferry sailing the Baltic Sea, is there a remote chance of a hazardous crossing? Yes to all.

The Baltic Sea has icebergs of all shapes and sizes which are frighteningly unpredictable! When there is a good stiff wind, which there usually is, they spin around like the teacups at Disneyland. Gale force winds are no strangers to the Baltic either. Wind delivers that chill factor to make it feel colder than it actually is. How cold does it have to get before "freeze to death" starts to become a real threat. Romantic? Mysterious? Magical? Not so much!

Remember, the punishing cold can physically wreak havoc. Frostbite works quite quickly. Hand warmers will not help. Don't bother with ear muffs. Your ears will fall off about the same time as your nose. Granted, cold weather gives you rosy cheeks but a good blusher from Revlon can do exactly the same. Finally, having frostbite nibble off your body parts is not the recommended way to lose weight.

KAYAKING

If a kayak is in your future, this is another warning to "proceed with caution." I speak from experience. Years ago, I — along with a group of friends — decided to vacation on the island of Maui. We all voted to stay at the Kaanapali Beach Hotel. It's a wonderful hotel right smack dab on the beach. Small and friendly is what you need when you travel. I dislike the hotels with 12 floors of elevators and bratty kids pressing all of the buttons. It can take a half a day to go up or down in a hotel when faced with pranksters like that.

The second morning, we gathered on the beach to make our plans for the day. The guys, two of them, had the schedule in hand. At 10 a.m., we could join in a beach volley-ball match. The females of the group, all four, decided we should take a vote. We asked the employees down at the pool who would be playing in the 10 o'clock match. Evidently, a group of girls attend each day and play the guests of the hotel. I asked if they wore t-shirts and shorts. Would we need to change?

"Hey, this is Hawaii, thong bikinis are standard" was the reply. Another perky employee added, "The volleyball on this beach is practically a blood sport. Most of the players are professional beach volleyball participants. Some are at the Olympic level."

My eyes spun around counterclockwise! I already could see my head being split open by a 60 mph spiked ball. Couldn't we just sit under a tree, sip pina coladas and make leis?

The employee offered several other options. Those activities which allowed us to stay partially clothed were what we considered. She did mention getting out into the ocean in kayaks. Her sales pitch also mentioned it would be an unforgettable and intense experience.

We agreed. It would be fun to paddle around in kayaks. The ocean was calm, and the waves were minimal. We promised each other that we wouldn't stray too far from shore. We dashed over to the kayaks and launched off from the beach.

It was a spiritual experience as we floated along. You're sitting in the ocean with just this little vessel between you and it. The sound of the water lapping against the kayaks is interrupted by the occasional squawk of a seagull. *Absolute serenity.* The kayak was an ideal place to meditate if you didn't close your eyes for too long, lose your balance and tip over, that is. I lose my balance quite easily so I just stared straight ahead. As we drifted further into the channel, we began to notice small ripples just a few yards away. With great relief, we identified a group of dolphins who began swimming around us. We were in awe.

Two hours into the kayak voyage, we all realized that we had made a mistake. We were paddling against the current. Our arms were cramping up! I figured any second I would have a stroke. Despite our efforts, we were getting farther and farther away from the shoreline. The waves were getting a bit more aggressive, the current was more forceful. Where in this Pacific Ocean were we going to end up? Directly across from Maui is the island of Molokai. Maybe we would wash up on the shore there. If we missed Molokai and continued drifting, the next land mass after that is Japan!

Then, from out of nowhere, we saw a boat which appeared to be headed straight toward us. It was the Coast Guard. I wondered how many stranded adventurers like us they rescued each day. They didn't let on that we were idiots, which was gracious of them. They were very kind, gave us lead lines to tow us back, and congratulated us for not being crushed by a humpback whale. *Hello? What was that?*

As it turns out, we were visiting Maui during the whale migration season. The humpbacks return to the warm Hawaiian waters. Also, during this time, dolphins have been known to tag along with the whales. So if you see dolphins, it's a pretty good bet that the whales are in the neighborhood.

Most people are familiar with videos of the whales "jumping" out of the water. The whale seems to appear from nowhere! It launches itself up and out, then slams back down. It's all quite theatrical! However, if anything is up there on the surface near the whale (a small boat, surfer, or kayaker, for instance), that "anything" will get knocked unceremoniously a hundred feet to the side and can become submerged along with the whale. The truth is that the idea of getting crushed by one of them isn't so far fetched.

One of the guys in our group wanted to recreate the kayak excursion the next day. He wanted to tempt fate. My idea of tempting fate is to eat a hot fudge sundae and see if it made me fatter. He wanted a close encounter with a whale and to risk his life doing it. He was serious. He was a dope. He intended to sit in a specific area and wait for lightning to strike, shall we say.

He was told where the whales migrate. Our friend even considered taking fish along as bait for the whale. He was advised that at least 100 pounds of fish may not even interest the whale. That is when he conceded defeat.

Instead, we went on the bicycle ride down Haleakala. It's a dormant volcano hundreds of feet up. It's eerily beautiful and offers a stunning view of the island. It takes a few hours to ride the 28-mile adventure. It's all downhill. If you careen off of the path, you land in lava. Nasty stuff. I was cautious. By the time I got to the bottom, my brakes were molten metal and smoking.

SPEED-DATING

This is a remarkable matchmaking activity intended to give singles an opportunity to meet new people – *fast*. It's called speed-dating. Based on first impressions, it grabs you out of your comfort zone and puts you in unfamiliar territory. I tend to be a pretty fearless person but I think giving up a kidney would have been less nerve-racking than this speed-dating venture!

These events are often sponsored by professional groups, churches and singles clubs. They're held in neutral locations, like a hotel conference room, church social hall and often on cruise ships. Usually, more than three dozen men and women, all strangers, line up on opposite sides of long tables. (Picture men seated on one side of the table and women on the other.) The gimmick is the brevity of each couple's encounter. For three to five minutes, the woman talks one-on-one with the man seated directly across from her. When the designated time has elapsed, people on one side of the table (the men or the women) move along to the next person. This rapid-fire type of encounter does require bravery. You must be stoic and remain on your best behavior even if you're talking face-to-face with the village idiot.

This is an interesting social experiment, and one of those instances when you ask yourself, *What do I have to lose?* You'll meet 20+ men during the evening. Sure, there's the good and the bad. God knows, there are the ugly! You never know about the participants. It's all very superficial.

These are strangers. That's why you always need to be familiar with the featured faces on that show *America's Most Wanted.* Are his pants baggy at the ankle? Could this be a sign of an electronic monitoring device? Ask questions. Don't be ashamed of being cautious! Here is an excellent one: "Have you ever been arrested or convicted of a crime?" Wouldn't you rather know that this gorgeous guy is a paroled ax murderer before you date? Also, how many life alert bracelets or necklaces did he have on?

When it comes to this trend in matchmaking, a good first impression and being a good talker are essential. The evening will go by in a blink, so pay attention. There's too little time to take notes. However, here are some tips that I found useful.

As he moves to the chair across from me, I don't stay seated. I stand to greet him so I can gauge his height. I then extend my hand for several reasons.

First, I evaluate the handshake. Is it a cold, warm or strong hand? Is it a firm handshake? Is this a hand you want to hold in the dark or is it like a squishy cup of pudding? Also, does he get out his hand-sanitizing gel after shaking my hand?

Also, as I extend my hand, I lean forward to capture his essence. Old Spice? Body odor? Bacon? Cigarettes? How about his breath? Is he wearing lipstick or mascara? I can't leave anything to chance because one guy actually had a car air freshener in his pocket. It wasn't just the string hanging from his pocket that gave it away. It was the stench of 24,000 Ponderosa pine trees in the immediate vicinity that made me step back, really far back, from this goofball. It's so sad when upon meeting someone your impulse is to puke.

As he positions himself across from you, make some sort of memorable statement or comment. Mention if you recently won the Nobel Prize. The main objective is to say anything that will make you unforgettable. This room is merely a sea of anonymous humanity. *You need to stand out somehow!*

Also, get to know him. He could be visiting earth from another planet. Ask him where he lives. Among the other more obvious questions you might ask are ones about work, if he is married, has children and pets. Other questions which I put on my list include:

> *Who invented the question mark?*
> *Would you prefer to play Mr. Potato Head, Twister or Trivial Pursuit?*
> *What is the scariest thing you've done?*
> *What is your favorite music, singer or band?*
> *Who is your favorite Muppet?*
> *What makes you happy and laugh?*
> *What makes you sad and cry?*

These speed-dating evenings are going to demand that you be aware of current trends, books and movies. I remember that years ago, everything was promoted using penguins. Penguins were wherever you looked. They were in toy departments as cuddly toys, in feature films, and in documentaries. Be aware that we have now transitioned to vampires. He may be into psychology and a fan of the new genre. He could be eager to discuss how we went from sweet, precious penguins to blood-sucking demons.

Since you're limited to up to five minutes, develop a strategy for your conversation. When you talk at a normal rate, you might say 80 words per minute. Do the math. Assuming you both will be talking, 200 words are all you'll have to use to say something witty. *Good luck.* Oh, and don't be yourself. You've been yourself all these years and look where it's gotten you.

In addition, before the evening begins, speed-dating participants fill out questionnaires as to what they hope to gain and what they expect to get out of the experience. In these surveys, the females tend to be more specific and reflective. Their goals: *meet an eligible man, professional, good-looking, good income, basically decent marriage material.* For the women, this appears to be serious stuff.

On the other hand, the men were … well, here's an example of the attributes they were seeking.

> *She should enjoy sports and be able to talk about the teams.*
> *She should be able to cook.*
> *She should look like a "Sports Illustrated" swimsuit model!*

Diminished capacity strikes again!

THE INTERNET

Your computer keyboard connects you with anyone —
anywhere, anytime. Is it conceivable that Prince Charming
is just a click away? Can you use the computer to find
true love?

The commercials for the dating services are so
darn wonderful. I want to weep. These magnificently
produced, 30-second vignettes give us a glimpse of the
couples who found each other through their service.
Actually, the little vignettes are screaming at us, *"This
could be you. But because you're such a procrastinator, the cute
guy in this commercial fell for her instead. By time you sign up,
no one will be left."*

I stopped putting it off. I joined an Internet dating
service. After reviewing numerous sites for about 20
minutes, I selected this particular dating service because
it seemed to be able to add a distinctively different layer
to my life. They offered scientifically researched questions, as well as all important psychological profiles to
successfully match up the right people. Wow! Sounded
good to me! Really, all I wanted them to do was to turn
my computer into a magnet for men. Within days, if
not minutes, my email would be jam-packed with men
looking for me! Thousands … hundreds …actually, just
seven would be fine.

Oh! Don't overlook their claim that more than 200
of their members get married every day! Spectacular

results, I must admit! Truth be told, I joined because they were offering a special discounted rate. The special rate was for "this weekend ONLY!" Their membership was on sale! My credit card was accepted. I was almost breathless as I watched the portal open up and invite me in.

I hastily filled out their questionnaire to pinpoint who I am. I didn't anticipate that part of the entrance exam to be so complicated. I am never sure who I am at any given moment. I pride myself in unpredictability. Next, I had to list my interests. I am interested *in everything.* No, not really. I hate that cage fighting stuff. Those guys should be out raking the lawn or doing something more constructive.

Wait. I didn't read the fine print because the sale had a catch. You could correspond with matches but not review photos. *Yikes! What good is that?* So I advanced to the next level of communication and paid a fee to accelerate the matchmaking process.

My goal is always "discernible intellect." *Ask questions. Get answers.* Meanwhile, you can't deny how convenient Internet dating is because you do this in the privacy of your home. You can sit there without any makeup on, eat chips, drink your Diet Dr. Pepper and belch. Or relax with a glass of wine if things are going well. Or even resort to a fifth of Scotch if who you are seeing or what you are reading is particularly dismal, and you realize that this may be all you have to live for!

As I reviewed my matches, I realized that checking their hobbies was important. I read that section first, as a matter of fact. Be leery if he enjoys quiet activities like turning the light switch on and off. Stanley's hobby was sleeping.

Software programs can manipulate anyone's photo into looking nice, cute or acceptable. From perusing the photos, it seemed that missing a front tooth or two is fashionable out there in the nether regions of the country. Some people don't even bother to touch up their picture. They were hit by an ugly stick and are proud of it. *Good for them.* They can go on about their lives and continue on the Internet Highway without me!

The obvious excitement of Internet dating is when the little photo icons begin to populate the page. It took amazing strength for me to open up that first one! "Who" would be staring back at me? Was I expecting to see a Denzel Washington or a Jon Hamm? The Internet matchups began to appear in their full glory right there on my huge, flat-screen display! Fully represented were various stages of hairdom — bald, balding and a combover. I was rendered speechless!

Owen from Decatur, Georgia, was in love with piercings — ears, lips. I don't want to know what other parts he's pierced! Oh, hey, here's Dennis from Wyoming. Evidently, Dennis got lazy because I think he used his most recent booking photo for the website. *Alert the media!* The other matchup I checked out is named Brian.

He's the clear winner because he writes that when he thinks, he gets a headache!

What group of men was I given? Was I matched by age, give or take a decade or two? One of the guys looked like his last job was heading up a wagon train. Maybe I was expecting too much. Nicer looking? Younger? But the more you participate, the more matches you will be receiving. I held off judgment until I corresponded with two of my matches. I needed to be optimistic and give this a chance.

Correspond? Evidently, again, I had a completely different definition of that word in my brain. Were they writing to me in English? Klingon? Incomplete sentences. Apparently, neither guy had been introduced to punctuation. *"Are you smarter than a fifth grader?"* Not these fellows.

Remember, by paying the membership fee, you can participate in the site's online groups, clubs, conversations, advice/discussion/opinion pages, and threads. The latest scientifically-tested relationship and self-improvement advice is emailed to you regularly. Honestly, how did I manage to function without all of this? Not well, I guess.

But was I a good candidate for this Internet dating/ relationship/matchup merry-go-round? The statistics support the theory that there are a few men my age who are still alive!

Internet dating has a certain momentum to it. It's an international escapade. I am making a concerted effort to stay on top of the emails. I am trying to deal with all of these opposite time zones in a coherent fashion because I have emails hitting my inbox 24 hours a day! It's a wonder that I can find the time to write this book!

I have spoken (I use that term loosely) with guys who have had nothing to say. They asked me *nothing.* Their answers to my questions were: *yes, no, I don't know, maybe.* Were they using flash cards to conduct this con- versation? Perhaps, they had gotten to a place in their lives where they'd used all of the words they know!

I am saving myself until I find that guy who sounds exactly like Kevin Costner with a French accent. Is this asking for too much?

Continuing on with further advice. I suggest you *do your research.* When a vague job title has been given, I pay close attention to how they describe their work or responsibilities. Just because he "travels a lot" doesn't necessarily mean he works on a cruise ship. He could work the carnival circuit. "Enjoys quiet moments and reading" could mean he is a well-read intellectual or someone currently serving time in solitary confine- ment. Getting to know someone these days takes on a whole new meaning.

We have access to public records so it's easy to find out if he's been divorced seven times, still married, bankrupt, and if there's a warrant for his arrest. It does get ugly sometimes. Dr. Phil has some of these scoundrels on his show every so often. Commit their faces to memory. When you spot them, turn and run!

Yes, connections happen. Sometimes a connection is made with someone who lives on the other side of the United States or the world. Who is going to go where? Will it be a long-distance romance or marriage and a move?

One dear friend met Mr. Cutie-Pie via the Internet, married him, and made the decision to move from California to the Midwest. She was leaving her family and friends. She was leaving a good job. She believed love would conquer all. *Yes, to a point.*

My concern was the Midwest weather. She was familiar with Southern California sunshine. She was unfamiliar with the words *"snow," "ice," "sleet," "frigid,"* and the phrase *"the temperature is below zero."* But this was only part of it. The exact location of her new home would be smack dab in the middle of Tornado Alley. I don't care that Southern California has earthquakes. The earth quakes, and basically your house is where you left it. It probably shifted a little, and it might be in a few pieces or on its side! A tornado picks up your whole house and deposits it … miles and miles away! Then you can't even go look for the house because your car has been blown away, too.

Wild weather update. So far everything has remained calm. She has no regrets. She continues to be madly in love and to be blissfully content in the middle of Tornado Alley. However, she confesses to keeping the Weather Channel on 24 hours a day!

SOCIAL NETWORKING

Everything I have written here will probably be obsolete in the next 10 <u>seconds!</u>

They're waiting for you — Twitter, Facebook, YouTube and MySpace. Then there's also LinkedIn and others! Some have pages and pages of photos, information, descriptions and opinions for the entire world to see. Don't overlook the intoxicating, addictive, interactive games like FarmVille. Some players go at it 24 hours a day! I suspect that special psychiatric facilities are being opened to treat FarmVille-itis. As the obsessed, cyberspace farmers are being led away in straight jackets, they can be heard yelling instructions to their loved ones ... *"Take care of the produce. The harvest is due. There's a bumper crop of broccoli!"*

My position with all of these sites is that they allow people to blab too much. Talking about what you're doing, who you're doing it with, and when. *C'mon.* Why do you need to let everyone know this? Plus, if you've got a good-looking boyfriend, why do you think all of your friends have to be in on it? No, they aren't deliriously happy for you. *They despise you.*

An exciting bonus with the Internet is the opportunity to be a bff to so many celebrities! Reading about what they're doing each and every day! He/she (yes, the actual celebrity) will text you to alert that a new message is coming your way! I shiver with anticipation. Everything is being updated in nano-seconds like when Paris Hilton runs over to Wal-Mart to buy a new toothbrush! It's only newsworthy if she uses a coupon. C'*mon.*

There are dozens, nay, thousands of dedicated Facebookers and MySpacers who spend most of their waking hours building their pages. They are intent upon showing you their world. It's an odd compulsion tainted with a smidge of exhibitionism that Dr. Phil is trying to cure on tomorrow night's show.

Moving around through Facebook, I happened upon Kevin, 42, from Oklahoma, who looks like Jerry Garcia. He was photographed in his room with Grateful Dead posters on the walls behind him. He admits his total surrender to all things Grateful Dead. However, his favorite song is listed as "Womanizer" by Britney Spears. His favorite color is aubergine. Am I missing something here?

How about someone who tweets that his herpes is in remission? What has happened to discretion?

In closing, understand the devastating effects of "unfriend." This happens when someone on Facebook removes a name/person from their page to "unfriend" them. This creates a stigma which can last a lifetime! The bond no longer exists. Access is denied. This may cause trauma. These unfortunate souls may even seek therapy or pursue litigation. *Next stop?* You guessed it ... Dr. Phil. Then again, if you "unfriend" someone, you could find yourself on *Judge Joe Brown* as the defendant in a lawsuit for the infliction of unnecessary pain, suffering and Internet humiliation.

Here's my word of warning to anyone wishing to put a photo on any site. As innocent as it seems, once that picture is out *there*, it is *there* forever. You can think you have deleted it. *Nope.* The original floats around in Cyberspace waiting for a new use. Like you might discover your beautiful, smiling face prominently displayed in advertising for frozen, Indonesian parakeet parts.

Tweet!

BLIND DATE

Most people cringe at these two words. *Wait!* This blind date thing could be great. Nice, educated friends want to introduce you to a nice, educated someone. They suggest a blind date. The first comment out of your mouth might be: *"Shoot me now!"* Think this through. This may not be all that bad.

The idea being promoted in this book is to experience all that you can. Do whatever is different. Keep in mind that your friends could be there to protect you and "guide" the evening. So don't be intimidated. Run off and read the book *Dinner Conversation for Dummies* and get dressed. What else were you planning to do that night? Watch *My Big Fat Greek Wedding* for the 53rd time?

I concede that your hesitation about the blind date is justified. It's shocking how many dolts are out there. It's lucky we aren't exposed to them on a daily basis. We would go screaming into the sunset. It would get really crowded out there!

You've probably heard about the guy who mentioned to his date that he was low on money. He asked if they could make a quick detour. It was to the blood bank! He "donated" blood for some cash. The blood bank was his personal ATM. He asked his date if she wanted to shove an IV in her arm for some cash, too!

Beware: Politics can incite unruly behavior. If a guy becomes a screaming lunatic during the most innocent of political discussions, watch out! If you try to segue to another subject, do so delicately. If he continues to rant during a mundane discussion about which dessert is the tastiest — pudding or tapioca, I would politely excuse myself and go home alone.

Sometimes there is a disappointment factor. He arrives at your door and just could not be any ... well, ickier. You are a decent human so you get through the evening being a kind and gentle soul. Remember, good manners will get you through the worst situations. That's why you graduated with honors from Miss Starling's Charm School.

$\mathcal{P}$LACES

THE OBVIOUS

While looking for Prince Charming, try to be subtle. Here are just some of the possibilities of places to conduct your search. Keep reading this section of the book for more ideas.

- **PTA**, unless you don't have children. Some regions allow you to participate even if you don't have children. Rent some!
- **Charities. Church.** Groups to participate in. Choirs to join. So what if you can't sing!
- **At the Polling Place, as a Voting Booth Volunteer.** This is one of the BEST places. Do your patriotic duty, and you'll be rewarded with the cleverest way to check out who lives right around the corner from you! Watch Mr. Voter as he comes in. As he signs his name, you make a note of his address. Plus, you can see on the official registration sheet whether there is a Mrs. Voter!

Hundreds of possibilities will pass through during the day. Check them out one-by-one until the polls close. It cannot get any easier!

- **Weddings and Funerals.** Do not pass up attending them. Multi-generational. Free food.
- **Concerts in the Park and Farmer's Markets.** Often sponsored by cities to encourage community interaction and participation. Hundreds of people with a shared interest. Go mingle!
- **Halloween Trick or Treating.** Superstition says that if you look in a mirror at midnight on Halloween, your future spouse will be in the reflection. You only get one chance at this in a year so don't fall asleep and miss it. Next Halloween I'm going to stare in the mirror and hold up a picture of George Clooney.
- **At Work as a Census/Survey Taker.** The census/city survey could be a way to find out who is in the neighborhood, too. Some cities conduct special surveys during the year to evaluate real estate development, current political climate, etc. However, this census/survey endeavor can be fraught with danger. Remember the census taker in the South who was hanged from a tree in the woods of Kentucky? He had the word "fed" scrawled on his chest. It wasn't with a felt marking pen either. It was something much more heinous. They are investigating whether the census taker was the target of anti-government sentiment. *Duh?!* If you decide to take on a census or survey, get life insurance before you start.

GYM

This is a perfect place to meet guys. I always am humored when the trainer suggests I'm there to "get back into shape." I have never been in shape. No doubt, the most depressing part of the gym check-in is filling out height, weight, measurements, etc. I told the trainer that, in order to find my waist, we'd have to dispatch a search party.

I glanced around the gym and was stunned by how beautiful bodies can look! Treadmills, weights, spinning machines, exercise classes, this was the place that would transform me. Every one of these pieces of equipment had been designed to maximize the burn. I could feel it. *When do I start?*

There, at the gym, nobody seemed to care about my skill level. Mine was at the bottom of the chart. But I promised myself that I would prevail and tried to conquer 5 minutes on the treadmill without going into cardiac arrest.

You may be the dedicated workout junkie who can find true love between the free weights, kickboxing, dance classes, aerobics, boxing or cardio-mix. A lot of clubs are open 24 hours. You don't want to miss someone who is lovely, eligible and yummy. But what happens if that person works out in the late evening or early morning? To casually run into this person, it could require you to stagger your visits throughout the day and night.

You may have to rearrange your work schedule or quit your job altogether.

SUPERMARKETS AND WAREHOUSE STORES

Find a fine fellow at the supermarket or warehouse superstore? *Why not?* But be careful.

The parking lot is a good place to meet a guy. As he drives in and parks, does he retrieve a cart from one of the outermost cart corrals before entering the store? Yep, that is considerate and thoughtful. Did he bring his own bags for the groceries? Going green is important, and here is someone who lives it! Don't be reluctant to talk to him whether you're coming or going. You may run into him again, and he'll remember how friendly you were.

There are different supermarkets and warehouse stores. Each one will attract a unique group of customers, depending upon location. In addition, there are the specialty, ethnic and boutique markets. After a few visits, you can determine which one has the most to offer. The environment and lighting are as important as who is in there.

Greenish florescent lighting is bright, harsh and hideous. If your makeup isn't perfect, you'll look like a vampire. Take the time to find those stores with "designed" lighting. You'll look perkier in those.

Shop elegantly and safely. First, if you use coupons, be organized. Be considerate. People can get hostile. If you're redeeming a fistful of coupons, don't inflict this kind of pain on shoppers when it's the busiest time in the store. If there is any decent guy in line behind you, chances are he's becoming annoyed. Burned into his brain at that very second will be your face with a big, fat X across it.

For hygienic purposes, don't place your purse in the section of the cart where the toddlers sit. *Think this through.* Those little crumb snatchers are placed here by moms and dads. As the parent shops, these diaper-wearing toddlers wiggle around, bounce up and down with their bottoms coming into direct contact with that seat. *Enough said?*

I must add a cautionary tip about cart contents. It's easy to reveal *way too much* about yourself if you're not careful. Cart contents can send dangerous signals. It's obvious that you shouldn't load up the cart with a pyramid of Ding Dongs and Twinkies. Don't buy the 10,000-count container of Tylenol either. Do you really have that many headaches? Need I counsel you on the very public purchase of lice shampoo? Large quantities of GasX is another terrifying signal for the average American! Exactly how unhealthy are you?

What's in his cart? You can size him up quickly. If it's filled with hair dye, nail polish and a case of Scotch, I would change aisles.

Some markets play great music. The specialty grocery store Trader Joe's celebrates Elvis' birthday, January 8, and rocks out with his music as an appropriate tribute. The rest of the year, it's always a musical treat while shopping there. Plus, the store has a wonderful atmosphere. The music is partly responsible for that.

I, along with a friend, dashed into a funky antique store a while ago. On the store's sound system was "Thriller." We, along with some other customers, started dancing down the aisle! What fun!! It was exhilarating! Pasadena, California. It happened here! Thank goodness life has unexpected whimsy.

Then there are those brain-dead stores which refuse to play music. Management and the legal staff have skillfully crafted a statement which they post at the entrance; *Music is not played in the store because it distracts the shopper.* Psycho babble. No, it's because they're cheap, and they don't want to pay for it. *Think about it.* They have decided, on your behalf, that you're incapable of shopping and listening to music at the same time. *Sure, no problem. I love to shop in a store if it feels like a morgue.*

At the supermarket, you may not have noticed the complexities of the product pricing. It's a ridiculous math challenge! You can buy 10 for $1.00 or 10 for $10.00. How about 3 for $5.00 and 7 for $12.50? To me, this might as well be calculus. Do they want me to have a nervous breakdown right there in the store? Of course, the next obvious question comes to mind. Do I need to buy all 7 in order to enjoy the savings? Don't forget that you need that member card, too! Or you save nothing! I find it to be discriminatory. Where does the ACLU stand on this one? Does it have to be this complicated? I'm forced to juggle my purse, a calculator, coupons, my list and a pen. The shopping cart should be redesigned with a desk top in place of that toddler seat.

*Please don't le*t me forget. You need binoculars! I can't read those signs all the way down the aisle. Can you? Also, in the warehouse store, you'll be directed to Row 97 for the pinto beans. Losing your way is not unheard of. To play it safe, put a tall, whip antenna with a flag on your cart so the rest of your shopping party can spot you.

Remember, a shopping adventure doesn't conclude when the groceries are purchased. It's vitally important that as he departs, and unloads his groceries into his car, to watch if he walks the cart to the corral instead of abandoning it in the middle of the lot. He's responsible for the cart until it's emptied and returned to the designated collection point. If he does walk it there, this speaks to his acceptance of responsibility. If he's divorced with children, he probably makes his support payments on time. That's probably part of some psychological study somewhere but I haven't bothered to look.

Before we leave the subject of warehouse shopping, please don't overdo it. Remember, the carts are larger and deeper than those at your average supermarket. There's no good gauge with these behemoths. Usually you figure it's time to stop shopping when you can't see over the four foot tower of muffins and frozen pizzas you have collected. You'll buy way more than you need. It's inevitable. Everything is a good deal. You're saving money; but when you visit the cashier to check out, the total will be equal to a first-class, roundtrip ticket to Paris!

Also, when you buy too much, this can play havoc with your social calendar. You will spend every available moment for the next month trying to figure out where to put all the stuff! I overdid it on a purchase of toilet paper one time. Luckily my neighbor allowed me to store 200 rolls in their garage. My garage was already stacked to the rafters with Costco canned food. I hope it doesn't expire too soon though or I'll be eating lima beans for breakfast, lunch and dinner.

The intention of shopping at the warehouse store is to buy in bulk to save money. Go there on the right days, and you can eat your way through the store on the samples. With all their products and services, they work hard to keep you as a customer. The "big box" store is there for you in life and in death. In fact, Costco sells wedding gowns and caskets! Reasonably priced, so I hear!

HOME IMPROVEMENT STORES

The testosterone can knock you over! These stores are filled with home improvement professionals and do-it-yourselfers. Aisles of guys are there! *Get going!* The "he" you are looking for could be measuring pipe in the plumbing aisle *right now*. At any given time of the day or night, these stores are packed with shoppers. The shoppers are there for a reason. It's not like at the mall where shoppers wander with glazed expressions. The customers in home improvement stores are an amazing array of laborers, designers, merry workers and (sometimes) single, unhandy men collecting parts for their very first project. Camaraderie is what you'll find at the home improvement store.

Don't overlook that yummy area — hand tools! Guys who use hand tools have strong hands and muscular arms. Something you may not even take into consideration is their ability to read. *They do!* They read, study and compare the features of the items on display. This is an excellent trait. It's a promising indicator that they probably read newspapers and magazines and watch insightful, informative documentaries, too. *Well, maybe.*

Home decorating! If you're in the "décor" department and spot a guy eyeing some chartreuse drapery sheers, I would admire his taste and strike up a conversation. There are good things to discover in

61

plantation shutters, ready-made and custom. It could mean a whole team needs to come to your house to measure. That goes for carpeting, too. Didn't you need a redo in that dining area? Could mean some handsome fellow out in the field needs to deliver personal service and stop by with dozens of samples for your perusal.

Paint! Another great department when you need someone to consult with to determine the best color. Should it be eggshell white or a butter cream? If there's a particularly good-looking employee in the paint department, you can come back day after day because you're redoing an entire house. Hopefully, you are, in fact, redoing something or you'll end up owning a lot of paint just trying to get a date. Point is — every room needs paint. Be selective in your colors so you give off an aura of class and taste. The paint adviser in the home improvement store will not be impressed if you elect to do the bedroom a day-glo orange.

Yellow is a popular color for a house — both inside or outside. I caution you now. Don't consider doing the exterior of your house a shockingly bright YELLOW. In full sunlight, that YELLOW can burn the retinas of squirrels. The last thing you want is to have PETA come after you because your way-too-bright YELLOW is harming squirrels and blinding birds.

Keep your wits about you. The possibilities are endless in the cavernous home improvement stores. You can wander for hours looking at men and their tools. Stay for the day. Take along a snack and refreshing beverage!

PARTIES

I have a friend who throws a party because it's Tuesday. These are not put together haphazardly. *They have themes*. Scenery is rented from prop houses. One catered affair was to be at a trendy club in Hollywood. Don't miss parties like this, even if you think the same people will be there or it's an inconvenient location. You'll have fun no matter what. *Go, make merry!*

For one such celebration, the party was on the second floor of the club. There was a problem. It happened to be an intensely hot day. It was more than 110 degrees outside. The first floor of the club was nice and cool, but then we walked over to the elevator. The door opened, my friend and I entered, and we were in a sauna. Evidently, the air conditioning on the second floor was not working! In mere seconds, sweat was pouring down our faces. Every cosmetic that I had put onto my face was now being absorbed by the collar of my trendy white shirt.

We glanced at the buffet table. It was pathetic. It had disintegrated into an unappetizing glob of goo. Atmospheric conditions being what they were and all

63

... you would be taking your life in your hands if you ate the potato salad. The bright spot might have been that the decorations in the room made up for the other casualties. Despite the party-giver's best intentions, they didn't.

There were hundreds of helium balloons. The heat had affected the helium so the balloons had descended from the ceiling down to a 5'5" level. You couldn't see the person you were standing next to let alone have a conversation with anyone several feet away. Any tall person had balloons circling their chest area. It was probably the most fun I've had at a party in years!

Of course, I couldn't find Prince Charming there. He was probably behind that bunch of yellow and green balloons way over there in the corner. We did consider popping the balloons but that would have been a sacrilege because the balloons were doing their job. They were floating in the air. They just weren't quite at the right height.

ALASKA

For decades, the ratio of men to women in Anchorage and Juneau was well publicized. Five men to one woman in the 1960s, I believe. It's about even now. If you're willing to venture into the bush, you'll continue to find that higher ratio. But hold on there before you make travel plans! You can't just drive your sweet mini-Cooper into the bush. You have to use a jet boat, Piper Cub airplane or helicopter.

You can run off willy-nilly to the post office with your change of address, but you need to resolve some important issues! We're talking Alaska bush here. Say it after me, "Tundra." Once "in" the bush/tundra, the means of transportation are snowmobiles and dog sleds. This is the territory where hunters go to search for moose, caribou, grizzly bear and wolves.

Maybe before you catch that flight out of *life as you know and love it,* you might want know some basic information? How far is the salon? Is there a Starbucks within a 50 mile radius? How cold does it get? Is there indoor plumbing? Gentle reader, this IS where the deer and the antelope play. Are you sure you're ready?

I can't fault you if you want to commit yourself to this adventure to seek "him" out. You will leave behind the pricey designer ski outfit. Parkas, plaid flannel shirts and bib overalls are the most serviceable. Build your skill set by scheduling rock climbing lessons, target practice at the rifle range, and cooking school for the wild game you and he will get, and that isn't all. He may invite you to go ice fishing. This is when you can experience what is called freezing cold, bitter cold … any and all variations of cold.

There's no argument — ultimate tranquility is on a frozen lake. But, I believe, ice fishing is as crazy an adventure as you can find. You either walk or drive out onto a frozen lake. You sometimes use a little hut that is set up for ice fishing or you will pitch a tent. A hole has to be cut in the ice and then the line is dropped in with appropriate bait, of course. You hope for the best.

Here's the *what if*. What if the temperature rises slightly, and the ice floe you are on begins to melt? *Yes, this happens.* The little ice platform begins to shrink. It's not as if you will float off to the North Pole. *Of course not.* You're in the middle of a lake. You are surrounded by land. Truth be told, *the ice you are on will melt, and you will slowly sink into the freezing cold water. Certain death?* I'd say you could count on it!

Your newly found Grizzly Adams guy may be wonderful, handsome, strong, protective … the best kisser ever … and maybe he's even done the Iditarod sled race 20 times. *So what?* Rely on your own instincts for self-preservation. Take along your cell phone and call the Ranger Station for a helicopter rescue. If you have access to a jet pack, take that, too.

If you want to book yourself a stay in testosterone territory, the greatest places to prepare — purchasing clothing, gear, and survival items — are the stores for outdoor and sporting goods. I recommend Cabela's and Scheels. The slogan for Scheels, in fact, is *gear, sports, passion!*

There you are! You want a hunk-a-hunk-a-burning-love? You just may find him there!

At the stores, you'll be shopping for hunting gear, guns, tents, golfing and fishing equipment, and much more in an out-in-the-wilderness atmosphere. The buildings are huge but they are so wonderful. Designed as an ultimate source for clothing, equipment, and outdoor gear, they are customer and visitor-friendly. Each has at least 200,000 square feet. But don't be confused about them being warehouse stores. You won't find the economy 40-pack of paper towels next to chain saws. These are places carefully designed for the outdoor aficionado.

I wandered wide-eyed from one area to the next. Huge aquariums were center stage with displays of taxidermy animals from around the world. I sat within three inches of a rhino. I was delighted! All displays are researched with dandy bits of information that will, I am sure, come in handy when I play *"Jeopardy"* the next time. Plus, at Scheels, you can ride a towering, indoor, three-story Ferris Wheel while eating their homemade fudge!

Both stores have demonstrations all day. These people know what they're talking about. You can go to ask for help on your golf swing. Learn how to properly clean your firearms. That skill is always handy. Cooking classes offer taste tests. You can benefit by attending a class on how to set up your Boondocks Blind (a camouflage enclosure that hides you when you're out hunting)!

These stores are like a Chuck E. Cheese for the outdoor addict — entertaining, excellent products, helpful staff and games to play! You should be able to enjoy an entire day's worth of guy-shopping here.

A HUNTING WE WILL GO

Be careful if in a moment of weakness, you decide to go along with something because "he" insists upon it. Is it against your better judgment? What should you do? I think we all know the answer to that.

My friend, Cara, was dating an avid hunter — *Mr. Outdoorsman*. We had all gotten to know him over the past few months. This guy knew everything sports and had done everything sports. He annoyed me but he swept Cara off her feet. They were an unlikely couple. Cara was debutante material. She could recite every color of the current OPI nail polish line along with every winner of *Project Runway*. Now, out of the blue and totally out of character, she was making plans to go deer hunting! *What? Shoot Bambi?*

It was hunting season, and Mr. Outdoorsman was going to bag his trophy buck. He did mention that his family ate everything they brought in — cleaning, butchering, cooking it, etc. That almost made her puke but my friend figured that she could be excused from that part.

He and Cara bought her gear. Pants, shirt, clunky boots and a vest were on the list. Expensive items but necessary for the outing. Cara was not pleased because the clothes were drab green and black camouflage and the vest was bright orange. She is very color-conscious and doesn't wear green or orange because they make her skin look yellowy. But Mr. Outdoorsman convinced her that this was the appropriate clothing. In fact, the orange vest would protect her from another hunter shooting her by mistake. Her big concerns up until that moment were the possibilities of twisting her ankle or breaking a nail. Now Mr. Outdoorsman had confessed that she might be shot by another hunter who flunked target practice.

The weekend came when the big deer hunt was to commence. I called Cara to wish her well. I was relieved to hear that she would not be carrying a loaded gun. My friend has trouble walking and chewing gum at the same time. If she suddenly stumbled, Cara could risk taking out a half dozen hunters if she had a loaded gun ready to go!

While on their hunt, Cara and Mr. Outdoorsman were out of cellular range. I didn't hear about the adventure until they returned. The first words out of her mouth were: "I broke up with him. He's a dope."

Here's what happened on their hunting date. Out in the wilderness, Mr. Outdoorsman found a perfect spot to set up. He would be on the ledge above a thicket. Cara would be 15 feet away sitting near some broken tree branches. As crazy as it may sound, Cara's job was to lure the deer to the area. She wondered if singing was involved, whistling or making deer noises. No, Mr. Outdoorsman wanted to spray deer lure onto her clothing. Deer lure smells like rotten apples. It's rank. It's foul and disgusting. He explained to Cara that she would be downwind or upwind or something (!) from him so the deer would be lured to the area. Insane? I am nodding my head "yes." Are you?

She said her response to him was: "You're an idiot, and that is the strictest definition of idiot, by the way. Are you from another planet?"

She insisted upon going home *immediately*. Then, as if this would make any difference, he tried to justify his behavior. His mom would always go hunting with his dad. She allowed herself to be doused with deer lure. Mr. Outdoorsman didn't think his request was unusual. He couldn't understand why Cara was upset!

Cara realized that this was not a match made in heaven. Skinning bears and plucking pheasants were not on her agenda. As kind-hearted as he and his family happened to be, she couldn't imagine a future which included deep-fried frogs and sautéed raccoons.

DOG PARKS

What about going to the dog park? If you don't have a dog, *rent one*. Dog rental agencies *do* exist. Go to the Internet to see if there's one near you. Find out where the nearest dog park is, and head over with your canine cutie so the hound can play with the other pups! Here's a group of people who are devoted to their animals. They're usually a friendly sort. The owners, not necessarily the dogs.

Here's another option for obtaining a dog. Your neighbor might appreciate it if you would take his/her dog for a walk or run at the dog park. Test the dog out, though. Make sure he's well behaved. The dog could drag you down the street face first if you aren't careful. A smaller dog can be easier to handle but could be a brat when it comes to interacting with other dogs. Try to know something about the breed. You have to be able to discuss the critter with the other people at the park. Don't look stupid. Be engaging and friendly.

Some of the bigger facilities offer dog parks with separate sections for little dogs, aggressive dogs and large dogs. Generally, they don't offer an ugly dog section. Sometimes they should to spare you from those breeding mistakes like a Chihuahua and a Mastiff. You can borrow different dogs and try out the different sections. The aggressive dog section could be scary. However, that may be the area with the highest percentage of male

71

owners. Take your pepper spray in case a pit bull looks at you like you're lunch.

Rules of etiquette are posted at the entrance. The idea here is to talk with other people, play with your pet, and supervise the activity. Don't sit texting or chatting on your cell phone the entire time. Remember the purpose of this outing. No, it is not to exercise the dog. *It's to check out the guys.*

And, please, don't forget to pick up the poop.

ELEVATORS

Yes, you can definitely meet eligible men in the elevator. The more rides you take, the more men you can meet. We should start with how unpredictable elevator environments are. The lighting is important. The greenish florescent tube stuff will make you look like a crypt keeper. Then there are the elevators with 5000 watt bulbs with reflective fixtures. It is so bright in these elevators, you need sunglasses. Furthermore, the lighting magnifies any facial imperfections. In fact, the lighting appears to enlarge your pores so you have skin that resembles the craters on the moon.

Mirrors in elevators can be helpful. If a good looking guy is in the elevator, you can study him carefully with discretion! It's usually tacky to stare straight at someone when they're just two feet away. This mirror-in-the-elevator technique is a stealth once over. Keep track of who gets off where. You can do a reconnaissance mission later on.

Due to unfortunate circumstances, the elevator can become your home-away-from-home sometimes. Yes, I learned that firsthand as I and two other passengers entered the elevator at the ninth floor lobby. Seconds after the doors closed, the elevator started to bounce. It wasn't ascending or descending. It was bouncing. The ground floor wasn't in our future for the time being so I summoned assistance. I thought the direct lifeline in the elevator was to the fire department. No, it was to the building's management office. My report was specific and was absent of any hysteria: "I and two others are languishing in an elevator that has turned into a carnival ride."

As I saw it, this was certain death. Yet we sat down in the elevator and patiently waited for someone to rescue us. Meanwhile, we all felt like baked potatoes because the 15,000 watt lights were on and pointed directly onto our heads. There was no ventilation. I could actually stand on my tiptoes and reach up to unscrew the lights but my fellow female travelers were terrified. They shouted, "Don't mess around with anything!" So I took my place on the floor and became increasingly irritated as the sweat poured down my face and onto my silk suit. I would have suggested singing songs but they were in no mood for that. They were terrified and crabby.

We had stopped bouncing quite some time ago. Even so, my fellow passengers' panic level continued unabated. It was absolutely silly. We were talking to our rescuers. Everything was under control. I was just anxious about WHO was rescuing us. I continued to hope for someone handsome and single.

In any case, they were going to stabilize the elevator, pry open the door, and we were to jump out *immediately.* We sat down while the elevator was maneuvered into position. When the doors opened, we had to jump down three feet to escape. Four firemen were standing there ready to help us. I went weak in the knees. Not because of this leap to safety. I looked at these four gorgeous guys and had heart palpitations!

Did I just die and go to Heaven? These were the most beautiful faces I had seen in years! Breathtakingly lovely! My heart went into some sort of rapid sequencing. I leaned forward and jumped into the arms of my rescuers. My condition did not require CPR or mouth-to-mouth resuscitation. *Darn it!*

I had a complaint after this obnoxious entrapment. I expected the building's management offices to have a little buffet for us since we were in there for several hours (or maybe it was only one). But no water, no chilled glass of Pinot Grigio. I don't understand why elevators don't have a "break glass in emergency" refrigerated cabinet with libations, imported cheese and crackers for occasions such as this.

REUNIONS

You romanticize. You can have great memories. The guy you thought was the cutest will now turn out to be the most hideous. Distance, by that I mean *years*, makes the heart grow fonder.

Reunions can be so tricky. Never an in between — either fantastic or horrible. You can tempt fate. Evaluate your intentions. Are you crazy or desperate? You get together with these friends/classmates from years and years ago. *What joy! What rapture at seeing them again!* You sit around and reminisce. You share fun stories, relive those escapades, and laugh about the pranks you pulled off. *What great memories!* Ten minutes later, you've run out of stories.

Now what?

CRUISE SHIP

You might like to try a cruise. Could be an unforgettable experience. *Mine was.* Not even electroshock therapy has made me forget my trip!

A good travel agent can guide you onto the right vessel for age, gender, singles-orientation, activity and sightseeing level. Consider the odds of meeting someone when up to 5,000 happy travelers are in close proximity to you … all floating in the ocean at that very moment. Newer ocean liners have a hundred decks or something like that. It's crazy! When you arrive on board, they give you a GPS tracking device to put on your belt.

Accommodations can range from a room about the size of a broom closet to luxurious suites. You can even have a balcony! Where would you ever be able to experience something like this? How wonderful — an unobstructed view of the ocean as you glide along! But be ever so cautious. Pack your binoculars because you always need to scan the horizon for pirates. *Sure! Could happen!* Too many martinis sent over to the Captain's table the night before, and he might execute one incorrect maneuver and guide the ship into treacherous waters with nary a warning.

It's obvious … however, I'll still point out that while on the ship, *you cannot be bored.* Spa, gym, beauty treatments, jogging, theater, pools, Jacuzzis, casinos, surfing, boxing, ice skating, climbing walls and plenty more. When all else fails, *eat.* You can eat *nonstop. They want that!*

They even schedule wake-up calls for buffets. The buffets are offered 24 hours a day. The midnight buffets offer different items from the daytime ones. For heaven's sake, you don't want to sleep through a free meal! Different people eat at different times. Who knows who will show up for that midnight buffet for one of those puff pastry swans with whipped cream? You can always sleep when you get home. *Get up. Go eat!*

The food should be listed as an activity. It's exceptional! It is every place you look! You'd never consume this much if you were at home. The intoxicating fresh air and *joie de vivre* allow you to toss your good habits overboard. *You will be possessed.* There's only one answer to this demonic possession. *Sea sickness.*

While working in Florida, some friends and I booked a day cruise to the Bahamas. It was one of those standard vessels. A few decks to make it seem like a true ocean outing. *Nothing fancy.* It was a beautiful spring day with a glorious light breeze. As advertised, we could anticipate two hours of sun and sea before we reached our destination. Our little group eagerly boarded the ship and decided to head to the forward deck. *This was the life.* We stretched out on chairs, closed our eyes. We promptly fell asleep. About 20 minutes into our excursion, we were rudely tossed onto the deck. The ship was pushing through some rough water and was sailing right into a storm.

I made my way to the railing, hung on for dear life as my knuckles got white, and the rest of me turned green. The bow was going up and down and up and down. The crew, with anxious glances, warned us to come inside. I quickly checked around for life boats, safety vests and rescue helicopters. I saw no life boats being lowered. No vests being distributed. No sounds of hovering helicopters. Were we going down with the ship? I've seen *Titanic*. I've seen the *Poseidon Adventure*. In both movies, the ships sank.

Was this crew fully aware of what are called Killer Rogue Waves? Those are 100 foot waves that come out of what appear to be normal storm conditions. You can be watching the horizon and suddenly a Killer Wave shoots into the sky. Could this ship withstand that kind of punishment? If not, we were all doomed. We were in warm ocean waters. If we didn't drown from the wave, the sharks that I imagined were already circling the ship would eat us.

My friends and I held onto each other as the crew led us off the deck and into one of the ship's lounge areas. The ship was being severely bounced around. You could not make headway by walking so everyone was crawling around. However, being inside the ship made things worse for me. It was claustrophobic. I could not breathe.

I was getting sicker and sicker. I looked into a mirror. I scared myself. My eyes were glassy. I was a deep shade of green. I could have introduced Kermit the Frog as my brother and no one would have questioned it.

My friends insisted I go for medical care because I could barely walk, focus or spell my name! I made my way through the crowded corridors to the ship's doctor. Other sick passengers had draped themselves across the stairways and couches. Passing this array of humanity was required in order to reach the lower level dispensary. Once I got there, I was told that they were all out of Dramamine. Now, how could this be? This was a ship. All they needed were two items in the medicine cabinet. They only administered aid to people who became seasick or people who had eaten too much at the buffet. Dramamine and Pepto Bismol. This was insane. The young, handsome doctor apologized and recommended that, since the "seas" were calming down, I should go to the upper deck and get some fresh air. I figured he was expecting me to throw up again and would rather I do it over the railing.

I did as he said. The sea was a bit calmer but I was still feeling queasy. I considered throwing myself overboard with a life preserver. They say when someone is seasick, they're not in their right mind. *That was me.* Well, I needed to put an end to this. Jumping into the ocean could be the answer. The Coast Guard would come to my rescue. Then it would only be a 10-minute copter ride to the hotel. Furthermore, none of the crew members mentioned when we would be out of the storm. *I panicked.* We were in the Bermuda Triangle, weren't we? This could be one of those storm systems where the ship completely vanishes.

Apparently, I wasn't all that seasick. I actually was thinking sensibly. I reasoned it out. If I did throw myself overboard, the Coast Guard could charge me for the rescue. Plus, I was wearing an outfit that required dry cleaning. One jump into the salt water, and my designer "casual wear" would shrink to fit a five-year-old.

Thank goodness that, by the time we docked in the Bahamas, I was feeling a lot better. We decided to enjoy our day by going sightseeing. As we disembarked, we noticed a booth on the pier promoting a tour where we would see the countryside, go to a town for shopping, and visit a quiet, white-sand beach. We chose that one. We wanted to see how the people lived, purchase hand-made items from a local artisan, and enjoy one of coun-try's most beautiful beaches! We all shouted in unison, "Sign us up!"

We drove by a grove of trees, then a pasture with Nubian dwarf goats and a building with a tractor. That was the countryside. Blink? You would have missed it. Our driver told us that we were stopping at a unique, one-of-a-kind gift shop next. (You may realize where this is going.) We stopped in at a small house with a table out in the front yard. On the table were purses and necklaces. Was it me or did I see these things at Wal-Mart the other day?

Finally, we were headed to the beach. Our driver dropped us off saying he would be back in three hours. We turned to look at this tropical paradise. It was a des-olate, deserted beach. No snack stand. No tables. No chairs. No vending machine with colas or candy. Oh, yeah, NO shade! We were in the Bahamas. Isn't that about seven miles from the sun? About one block away from the Equator? It was blistering hot. We were going to get horribly sunburned. As tourists, we have such high expectations of these tours. *What were we thinking?*

By the time we returned to the ship, we were eager to be heading back to Miami. However, we were still apprehensive about hitting another storm. While boarding, we asked a crew member about the weather. He reassured us that conditions were perfect, and then he invited us to enjoy our return voyage by visiting the ship's evening buffet. We all looked at each other and ran off to the dining room.

It was extravagant. We evaluated the offerings. We started with the desserts. Puff pastry swans with whipped cream — one of my cruise favorites. We moved along to éclairs. Next up, cherries jubilee. We could not stop. *Everything was luscious.*

After another hour of stuffing our faces, we waddled to the upper deck. It became imperative that we have visual confirmation that Miami was on the horizon. We felt ecstatic. We were less than a half-hour away. To me, it seemed like the Promised Land.

I know you'll think I sound dramatic but that cruise almost killed me. But I learned an important lesson. In the future, I will be prepared. I will pack Dramamine, a life jacket, clothes that won't get ruined if I have to jump into the ocean, shark repellent, and an umbrella in case I get stranded on a beach with no shade.

BACK TO SCHOOL

Meeting men in a class at an adult school is brilliant! You attend because you want to learn something and broaden your horizons. He's there doing the same.

I recently signed up for a session to focus on the harmonica. This wouldn't be just any harmonica. This was a *blues harmonica* class. I imagined myself getting really good at it and performing around town. I visualized intense practice sessions and taking in all of that crazy club energy. I was on my way to becoming a phenom.

Here's the scenario, and I have thought this through.

The Rolling Stones are in concert here in LA. Mick has a cold sore and cannot play his blues harmonica. They will need someone to step in to help him out. Weeks after finishing my class, I sent the Stones (via Priority Mail) my Blues Harmonica Certificate of Completion along with my phone number and email.

The Stones won't be on tour for a while, but I'm positive Mick put my information in his Blackberry.

See how easy this is? I could be getting a text any day!

TELEVISION

Do the math. How many channels are there? How much programming do we need? How many shows have men on them? Sports, Entertainment, Reality, Game Shows with hundreds of men in every possible circumstance and situation. Hundreds of men ... right there in your living room! *Turn on the television! Honest!*

I know of celebrities who have contacted news anchors or reporters as well as contestants on shows which resulted in dating and, honest to God, marriages! What about considering a *Jeopardy* contestant as a potential husband? *Why not?* You can write a letter to him through the show. The production company will forward it to the person, unless the address is written in big block letters and the envelope is sealed with pieces of chewed gum. If the contestant mentions being married, don't waste the stamp. But single? *Who knows?* You may only end up with an intelligent pen pal but worse things have happened.

So, let's review what a *Jeopardy* contestant is like. We watch them, admire them, and envy their intelligence. But notice something else.

"I'll take Political Buffoons for $100, Alex, please."

Unbelievably polite! Is that amazing? Is that special, or what? They all look scrubbed clean. Most likely they have clean fingernails. They have exceptional intelligence because they can form the *answer* into a *question.* Try to do that in your daily life. People will think you're positively charming. *Maybe not.*

Participants on the reality shows? I'm talking about the "talk" type reality shows like what Jerry Springer hosts. I'm sure these folks pick their noses as they drive their cars. Do they know what etiquette is? Snake tattoos on their forehead? Have these people been born and raised in areas where atomic bombs were tested?

Adventure/reality shows are a different story. Contestants need to qualify and exhibit a competitive nature. The producers create little back stories to give us insight as to who they are. We can observe their behavior as the weeks progress. Is the person kind, ingenious or funny? *So why not send a fan letter?*

The other side to this television thing is for *you* to be on it! Remember, everyone gets to have their 15 minutes of fame. Give some thought to how you might wish to accomplish that! Fifteen minutes of fame is due everyone because it's an unalienable right. I think it's in the Constitution.

If you're thin, bulk up to get on *The Biggest Loser.* But don't get carried away with that bulking up. If the show rejects you, your next stop will be Sumo wrestling!

America's Got Talent and *American Idol* are perfect for getting discovered. If you don't have any talent, that could be a problem. Now I say "could be" because sometimes they enjoy the occasional fool and give them plenty of exposure throughout the season. The idea is to get you out there. Learn to yodel. That's a good start!

My television debut was on *The Tonight Show with Johnny Carson.* This was some years back but it was a life-affirming moment and has gotten me great notoriety. You never know, however, whether silly moments like this will affect my chances of ever receiving the Nobel Prize.

There I was standing in line outside the NBC studios in beautiful, downtown Burbank waiting to attend a taping of *The Tonight Show.* An hour before the taping, a man sprinted out of the building and began waving his hands to get our attention. He introduced himself as an assistant producer. *WOW! Celebrity adjacent.*

He got our undivided attention when he announced, "Tonight you could become a star. We're going to play Stump the Band. This is when we have someone in the audience challenge the band with an obscure song, which they, of course, have to sing. If none of the band members can guess it, you win a prize. So, does anyone have a song they want to try?"

My hand shot into the air because this would be my chance. This was the rare occasion when preparation meets opportunity. I felt ready. *I could be twenty-four hours away from stardom,* I told myself. *Even my own series! I will be discovered tonight!*

I sang three tunes, none of which were entertaining enough to qualify. Then divine inspiration came. *I would make one up!* This was to be my television debut, and I could not let this chance pass by. I made up some lyrics, and waved frantically for the assistant producer to return to me for another audition. I think he knew that I had the potential to make a fool out of myself.

He listened; smiled and said, "You're in."

The participants for Stump the Band were led as a group into the studio. I was directed to the third row, aisle seat. This was excellent. The reason I even went to this particular show happened to be to see Tina Turner. Fate had smiled on me.

During the second commercial break, Johnny Carson walked up into the audience. The camera angled toward him, a cue was given, and we were on. He welcomed back the television audience, introduced the Stump the Band segment, and turned to ask if anyone had a song. I was poised and ready.

I yelled out, "Me, me." He asked me for my name, where I was from and the title of the song. He mimicked the title and gestured to the band. Naturally, they didn't know it because the song was scarcely an hour old. They made a good try but eventually it was up to me to sing it.

Johnny looked at me and said: "Your turn." I realized that this was my moment. The world was waiting.

I began my composition to a familiar tune ... "Bagel Benjy Bagel Benjy, how's by you? How's by you? Selling kosher pickles, three are for a nickel. Sell me two. Sell me two."

Johnny blurted out, "We've been had."

Well, friends, family and millions of strangers saw me. Maybe even YOU! I was on national television. I co-starred on the show with Tina Turner! I saw her up close but there was never an opportunity to exchange names and addresses for our Christmas card lists.

But here's an exciting postscript. I will receive second billing when the DVD of the show is released. Tina, of course, will be the headliner with The Stump the Band segment listed after her! That will be me!

Bottom line is how quickly this can happen. Plus, this is ridiculously easy. Game shows, reality shows and funniest video shows — consider all the possibilities! *Dog the Bounty Hunter* is not one I would recommend but if you're wanted and jump bail, his show could make you famous.

Survivor is another great vehicle, unless you get dumped in the first episode. The person who gets tossed off is usually an older woman who is not wearing a bikini. But even that person gets a paragraph in *People* magazine. *Think about it.*

How about *The Price Is Right?* I'm always fearful about that big wheel. The excitement builds for that Showcase Showdown but to get there the contestant needs to spin that cumbersome wheel with the dollar amounts. The host cautions the contestant to step back after pulling on it to get it spinning. Sometimes I have to catch my breath! *Scary!* Itty-bitty people have to give it a huge yank, and I've seen contestants almost tumble underneath it! As they stand up, the wheel is now whizzing around inches from their head. I don't think anyone has had their head split open though. My advice? Be careful if you make it to Showcase Showdown.

Don't be too vain to pass up a television appearance. There may be a time when you're invited to appear on a national TV show, but you hesitate. Well, how stupid would that be? Pretty stupid considering I did it.

My company Art on the House, Inc., was invited to present its product on a popular home-shopping channel. I along with my business partner, Rich, were to be on a segment demonstrating how our Country Series Kit can help you turn dull, boring walls into exciting works of art.

Believe it or not, Rich handled it alone. What was my reason for not appearing on camera? That particular day, I thought I looked bloated. I can be such a dope.

That decision is even more ridiculous when you consider the audience! For the most part, the viewers were sweet little old ladies with cataracts who can barely tell the TV from the microwave oven.

AIRPORT SECURITY

It's nice to stand out in a crowd. I enjoy it, anyway. I'm not including airport security in that statement though. Blending in is critical when it comes to this particular crowd. *I don't.* For some reason, I look suspicious, guilty or way too nonchalant. Those are the signs of someone who is in possession of contraband.

While I was traveling with Rich, we were faced with a second security checkpoint before being able to board our flight. It turned out that he was not to be subjected to this, but me. I was picked out as a test subject, I guess. As usual, Rich walked some distance away in case I was to be incarcerated. While they would be cuffing me, he could then claim never to have known me and continue on alone.

At times, Rich sees his association with me to be jam-packed with dangerous unpredictability.

Please understand right here and now ... I agree with safety and security. For example, I have childproof locks on drawers in my home. My daughter is in her teens. I don't leave anything to chance.

I now have been told to move forward to a special desk for a further search and to be interviewed! Naturally, I have gone into my own little make-believe world about this search. Some handsome officer would be interviewing me. Someone like Liam Neeson. He could meet me, fall in love with me. *Yeah, sure, Anita.* Keep in mind that this was Cincinnati and not Paris. In mere moments, I came back to reality. It did turn out that I was to be a guinea pig for the new security checkpoint officer — Officer Darlene.

She started with my purse by dumping out all of the contents. Thank goodness I wasn't transporting my Waterford that day. It would have been shattered to bits! I was asked to identify the items on the table. I named them as requested.

"This is my Hello Kitty Spotty Dotty wallet, Maybelline Great Lash Mascara, Maybelline Mineral Pressed Powder, Revlon lipstick called "Stop Me Now," a book *How to Make Insanity Work for You,* BIC ballpoint pens, a magazine called *Crazy for Crafting,* still camera, video camera, notebook, Oil of Olay Ever Lovely hand lotion, comb, prescription eyeglasses, Ray-Ban sunglasses, LA Dodgers baseball cap, moist towelettes, crumpled wads of paper, tissues and, of course, our survival food — an unopened, three-pound bag of peanut M&Ms."

Darlene took the unopened, three-pound bag of peanut M&Ms and studied it. Yes, an unopened, three-pound bag of peanut M&Ms. I became perplexed. What could be the problem? I was very serious when I explained to Darlene why I had this item in my purse. (Furthermore, I was NOT about to open the bag to share some with her either.)

"If we crash somewhere in the Rockies, Rich and I would need survival food until we were rescued. Remember those soccer players in South America whose plane crashed in a remote location? No one could find them! They had to resort to cannibalism. Well, I refuse to let that happen to us!"

Then, they began the metal detector wand search of my body. All was fine with my feet, shoes, knees and thighs. If they had been using a fat detector on my thighs, the device would have shorted out.

The metal detector went to red alert level as it ascended toward my chest area. The wand began emitting a loud beeping sound. I expected red lights to start swirling overhead accompanied by ear-piercing sirens filling the terminal. The entire uniformed group observing this search went pale. Was the wand detecting a gun? A knife? I had been pleasant and cooperative, but I bet in Security School they warned them about people like me. Sweet, cooperative, kind … then suddenly they SNAP!

I explained in a friendly tone, "My bra is a sturdy underwire garment made by the United Steel Workers. All metals, fabrics and fibers are super strong and create a super structure. It's much like the technology behind that which supports the Brooklyn Bridge."

I turned around with my hands in the air like Heidi Klum on the runway. I smiled and waited for their response. Needless to say, this was sheer entertainment for my fellow passengers, and they were straining forward to hear more of the security shakedown.

Evidently, the security guards were either humored or convinced that I wasn't a threat. They allowed me to proceed without a strip search. Rich was relieved that I didn't cause a scene and get dragged off to airport prison. We boarded the plane without further incident.

I didn't mind being a test subject. You know, it was for the greater good of the country. But I thought I should have gotten a souvenir of some type. A little pin announcing, "I've been searched" as a keepsake perhaps?

As it so happens when you're the center of attention, people gravitate toward you. It's an easy way to strike up a conversation because they feel they "know" something about you. Rich and I were fortunate to be in First Class, so that immediately separated us from the great unwashed.

A good looking, middle-aged man stopped by to talk with me. It was an exquisite delight to meet his acquaintance! Slightly southern accent. Infectious laugh. We had a great conversation but then realized we lived states away from each other. He did not travel to L.A. often, and, sadly, he lived in Albuquerque. There's no chance I will visit that city again.

I was in Albuquerque several years ago. While in the downtown area, I saw a group of tarantulas walking down the street. They were in a lock step formation like in a parade. They were as big as beavers. With creatures like that roaming free, how can you safely wear open-toe shoes? It was simply awful. Reason enough never to go there again.

NOTE: I have traveled by air but was not subjected to the body scan. Although, I wonder how discreet they are when celebrities go through. Somebody is going to find a way to capture those images and send them out to the Internet. You wait. It's going to happen. I check TMZ.com every day, as a matter of fact!

I, however, am looking forward to the feel-you-up-let-me-poke-you-there procedure. I will try to go through twice if it's a good-looking young man handling this part of the security checkpoint. I recently learned at the end of the feel-you-up-let-me-poke-you-there gauntlet, they have installed a tip jar!

ℋOME SWEET HOME

YOUR WELCOME MAT

When he comes to visit, be proud of who you are and what your residence represents. Macaroni and popcorn artwork should not be displayed on the refrigerator unless done by you in therapy. Animals and children should be well behaved. If not, call in that cutie "The Dog Whisperer" Cesar Milan and get a two-for-one deal.

If you meet the boyfriend's offspring, and they remind you of the kids in *Children of the Corn,* don't go on a second date. You may even have to change your name and move! The word "creepy" is in our vocabulary for good reason! This is one of them!

Trust your instincts. Also, as for décor, you may want to consider donating your Elvis paintings on black velvet to The New York Museum of Art. As for those black light posters in your bedroom, it's time to send them on their way.

If he's staying for something to eat, have decent dinnerware and flatware. I have visited friends who have forks with tines that are bent and going off into different directions. You bring the fork up to your mouth, and one tine is poking you in the nose. Their knives serve no useful purpose. They've been used as screwdrivers over the years. When noticing this, I always hope my host is serving something that doesn't need to be cut. Soup is good.

Be cautious about the inexpensive home décor items like candles. A sweet friend of mine was entertaining and had a beautiful display of candles throughout her apartment. When he rang the doorbell, that was the cue for her to run around and light them. As he walked through the door, the apartment was in the process of catching on fire!

The candles were made of wax but water must have been mixed in with it. The lit candles were spitting sparks. The tablecloth was on fire. The carpet was on fire. A fabric wall hanging was on fire. *It was a disaster!* They took saucepans and threw water everywhere. The romantic moment of the candles lasted about five seconds. The smell of smoke lasted about four weeks.

Several months ago, I finally decided to have a dinner party. I thought I would invite some adult types who are good for conversation and very forgiving if I ruin the meal. I hesitated in the past because something like this requires confidence. This was not a children's party.

A children's party is simple. Have the children do some crafts, jump around in an inflatable spaceship, and eat cake.

Whether I host a children's party or a large gathering of friends for a casual barbeque, I use large plastic cups. They are lined up on the counter ready to be filled with a refreshing beverage. Each guest has their own cup with their name on it. I never ever neglect to put one special cup out. The heads-up came from the *National Enquirer.* This individual was frequently spotted through the country. He is dead but the rumors that he still lives persist. A cup with "Elvis" is always included. I figure stranger things have happened. He could be in the neighborhood, spot all of the cars, see the party in full swing, and walk on in!

My dinner for adults would need a carefully-thought-out menu, place cards, china, crystal, and that all important Martha Stewart stuff. It wasn't until the day before the dinner that a friend asked if I had polished my silverware. *MY silverware?* I honestly *forgot* I had real silverware. If I can *forget* that I have real silverware, I must have forgotten about bank accounts somewhere! I'm checking with the State of California for Unclaimed Assets next!

The dinner was a success. I was relieved that at no time did the smoke alarm go off. I was complimented on my delicious lasagna. (It was Stouffer's. I figure why should I make it from scratch when they already do such a nice job.) Everyone was surprised with how beautifully everything came together, considering my apprehension. But I wasn't about to rest easy. It takes several hours for food poisoning to kick in. I prayed that I didn't contaminate anything by accident!

If you're planning a dinner at your home, review the contents of your medicine cabinet and clear out the laxatives. Get rid of the embarrassing drugs and potions. When your guests use your bathroom, they're likely to check what your medicine cabinet will reveal. The most innocent of products could be on the shelf, but that doesn't matter. People misread and misinterpret.

What's even worse is when they assume you have some wretched disease because of something they have discovered by seeing a little vial after they moved the aspirin bottle over to the right. Don't allow this to happen. It's totally preventable because these assumptions can become a huge, huge mess.

Your guests may be friends but there's sure to be a gossip monger among them. That person will be eager to leave your home and begin to Tweet. Without your knowledge, an outrageously, incorrect health history could be out on the Internet before your dishwasher has hit the rinse cycle.

Towels in the bathroom. Please have little towels, whether cloth or paper, for guests to dry their hands on. It's criminal to have them turn around to the rack behind them to wipe their hands on a bath towel. Exactly where has that bath towel been?

If you have any personal letters or notes lying around, put them away. Be sure to hide any of those FINAL NOTICE bills if you have any. You cannot leave them in plain sight. If it reads, "This is an attempt to collect a debt," throw it under your bed. Just remember to retrieve it later or you, inadvertently, may have your car repossessed. You will absolutely, positively scare off anyone if they see evidence that you're a deadbeat. Worse yet, they may think you'll be hitting them up for money after you serve them the apple crisp dessert.

DÉCOR

Do you decorate your home for yourself or for Prince Charming? What do you put on the walls? Those Burger King posters aren't considered art. What's on your coffee table? Resin grapes and wax fruit? Are your couches held together with gaffer's tape? Mine are but you'd never know because I have shabby chic slipcovers. Four years ago, the legs on the couch broke. I couldn't bring myself to throw the couch away. It sits on sturdy concrete cinder blocks now. Perfect solution!

I'm very sentimental about my "inherited" furniture. My criticism is that the legs and arms on the chairs are wobbly. Billy Bob Thornton is afraid of antiques. He has some type of phobia about them. This is probably why. You can sit on a magnificent-looking 100-year-old chair, and it will collapse underneath you. *Traumatizing!* However, Super Glue can fix the problem. Indeed, I was forced into action when one of my chairs collapsed underneath me. The legs went completely flat, and I crashed to the floor. I headed off to the hardware store to purchase the giant-size Super Glue.

Well, the Super Glue was purchased. I don't tend to read directions. I like to jump right in. On this occasion, it probably would have helped me ... *a whole lot.* I spread a good dollop across the chair legs, then put more in the holes and pushed the pieces together. Without realizing it, my fingers had slipped right into the glue. I was stuck. I could not pull away. I was now officially part of the chair. I became terrified. Was I doomed to spend the rest of my life as part of a maple Captain's chair?

Dragging the chair with me, I crawled to the phone. I called a friend for help. Luckily the first person I reached said he would be right over. I could hear him laughing before he hung up. Upon arriving at the house, he was still laughing. He asked me for my nail polish remover and proceeded to pour it onto my fingers. Soon I was free! I felt so relieved. I started to cry.

I know someone who tried to loosen the cap of some Super Glue with her teeth. She pulled on the cap and squeezed on the tube. Yep, the cap came off but the Super Glue squirted across her lips and into her mouth!

The 911 team was summoned and off she went to the ER. *Moral of these stories? Super Glue can be helpful, but be careful when using it!*

Back to décor ... Is your bedroom inviting or do 10,000 plush toys live there? How about plants? Flowers? Has that silk flower arrangement been over there on the dresser since Clinton was in office? A tumbleweed with spray glitter over there in the corner doesn't count as minimalist art, either. Or, Southwestern art for that matter!

I'm very forgiving when it comes to bathrooms. I think they should be crazy and fun. Most guys have bathrooms that are so dirty you can't figure out if the walls are garden green or just caked with mold. I have monkeys on my shower curtain. If that doesn't seem very adult, I don't care. It gives me pleasure every time I look at it. I expect the same from any guy I am dating. Otherwise, please, why bother?

CLEANING

Dust on the tabletop is not a crime against humanity. I think a thick layer of dust is simply evidence that the environment is being spared from excessive aerosol furniture polish vapors. Fewer paper towels are being thrown into the trash, and far fewer dust cloths are sucking up electricity when they are thrown into the washing machine and then into the dryer. I prefer more indiscriminate dusting.

As the dust builds up on tables, my daughter writes messages to me. "I love you, Mommy" means more to me than seeing my face in the reflection of the high sheen from incessant polishing! I believe my theory of anti-dusting is helping to delay global warning.

A very clever young mother I know came up with the most ingenious way to get her boys to help with cleaning. Keeping her young twins busy and playing together peacefully required strategy. After all, toddlers usually have the attention span of gnats. But she noticed their complete concentration when she vacuumed. They were transfixed by what messy stuff was on the carpet, and then how it magically disappeared after "that machine" passed over it! They both wanted to use it. Well, this high-performance, super-duper vacuum cleaner was way too big for the boys to handle. It would have them flying through the air as it flew through the rooms! Plus, with the two of them, there would be a pesky issue of sharing.

Why not give each boy a simple, lightweight, portable DustBuster! The boys were ecstatic! For years, they proudly used their appliances to make the messy stuff disappear. They became vacuuming connoisseurs. The outrageously expensive transition came when they discovered something totally innovative on a television commercial. This product had unique features their

Dust Busters didn't offer. They each asked for a Dyson Ball Vacuum Cleaner for Christmas! *They got them!*

Of course, you want your house to be presentable when he stops in for dinner. But how much cleaning is necessary? Who's setting the standards? First, if you have children, make sure all chicken nuggets have been removed from between the cushions on the sofa.

It takes time to dust properly. It's not merely those table tops. You have to dust the pictures, items on the wall, and whack those cobwebs out of the corners way up there above your head.

Don't overlook polishing those faucets in the kitchen and bathroom. They should dazzle.

Wash the floors and don't forget the windows! Are you completely exhausted now? Save yourself a lot of grief. Take him out for dinner. *You pay.*

It's expected that females have a tidy, clean home. Men, on the other hand, are excused if their place looks like a landfill with rotting vegetation in the refrigerator or on the counter *Scrubbing Bubbles* may run away in fear upon glancing at the soap scum buildup in the bathroom!

Don't be surprised to learn that archeologists are conducting a dig in the accumulated dust and dirt in his living room. They suspect something is buried down there circa the Paleozoic Era. Take a seat and check out what items they unearth. Radiocarbon dating may even be necessary.

If you have a chance to check his kitchen, try to figure out how long it's been since he's washed the dishes. Maybe it's perfection. Usually it's not. But benefit of the doubt, let's hope there aren't more than 20 dishes and cups in the queue. Also, what about the stove? Does it look as if the food blobs spilled on it require a blow torch to remove them?

When visiting his place, keep this in mind. Messy is a miserable character trait. Not to be confused with dirty, though.

CHILDREN

Do you have children? Are they obedient and respectful? If the children don't behave, don't date. That goes for you and for him.

Too many relationships are jeopardized because of insufferable crumb snatchers. You don't dare threaten children into good behavior because they will speed dial Child Protective Services on the cell phone you gave them. Let's hope you've done a Dr. Phil type job of raising your children, and they won't be sneaking around taking pictures of you and the boyfriend, then posting them on the Internet.

Kids will disclose things about you that you wish they would forget. You could have the body of Pamela Anderson, and your kids will still make disgusting remarks to their friends. Remember, one little trauma in their lives and they are screwed up forever. You know that, don't you?

For example, my daughter reminded me of a lullaby tape played at bedtime when she was a toddler. It was a beautiful melody, and throughout the song, the singer would call out her name. She said that while she would be falling asleep, listening to the music, a strange voice would echo through the darkened room. *"Christina, Christina."* She would frantically look around. Did a stranger enter when I had walked out? This stupid lullaby tape was terrorizing her!

It freaked her out. It still upsets her today. In fact, ever since then, she has insisted upon flood lights in her bedroom. However, she is comfortable with a 150W bulb which remains on all night and a motion sensor alarm. At one time, she wanted a private security guard. Thank goodness I talked her out of that.

See how ugly this can get?

PETS

There's no guarantee that Prince Charming will like your animals. While getting to know him, you'll discover if he is animal-friendly. But to proceed with caution is an understatement.

How many animals are in your household? Is there a dog that you dress up? Is your cat one of those creatures that you have nonstop conversations with? Parrots and myna birds have been known to drive people nuts. Little kids always want (and usually have) hamsters. They want to share their little pal with anyone who comes to visit. Hamsters bite and are known to mutilate noses. With animals, a relationship can come to a screeching halt. Canaries, dogs, cats...I will start with cats.

He may not mind a cat. But two? Three? Four? A multitude of cats doesn't make you more desirable. It could be a curse. *Sorry.* Your kind heart may do you in. You need to practice saying, "No." Sure, there are those sad circumstances when a friend is moving and the new place doesn't allow animals. *Could you take the cats?* she asks. Say, "NO." Or a friend is dating a guy who's allergic to cats. *Could you take the cats?* Again, your answer could be "NO." But you, soft soul that you are, welcome the cats. You're such a lovely friend. *Stupid?* If your house has 100 rooms, I guess that adopting a few dozen cats might work out beautifully.

So I say, *don't feel guilty. Don't feel obligated.* Animals can live for decades. Remember, you're the one who breaks out in a sweat when you're asked to commit to a one-year gym membership! Your response to anyone offering you any type of pet must be an unequivocal "NO!"

I love cats. I have three because I couldn't say, "NO!" They were inherited from my daughter. One shocking detail that you may learn after agreeing to the new furry roommates — these are *inside cats*. Declawing is not part of the vocabulary here. Does the phrase "Cat Lady" make you shiver? *Hello!?*

How about insisting upon a kitty trust fund? Those people who are giving you the cats should understand the future expenses and hardships you'll be facing! Besides the shots, food, kitty litter, and mandatory toys, there are countless other expenses. Oh, oh, oh, don't let me overlook that special, outrageously expensive flea medication. This medication may be expensive but trying to avoid that purchase by making family members wear flea collars as ankle bracelets will *not* do. Don't even entertain the idea of handing them out to your guests either. Refinance the house and buy the Frontline.

In no time at all, lovely decorative accents like chenille throws will be used to camouflage the hideous condition of your furniture. Emphasis on that first syllable ... *FURniture.* Underneath the throws is the evidence that cats with claws live here and have taken over. Chairs and couches have been ripped to shreds. Everything looks like scratch poles. Destruction reigns supreme. Upholstered furniture is a thing of the past. I speak from experience. I have sprayed water at my cats to retrain them to stop the destruction of the sofa. I have only managed to turn the living room carpet into one giant Slip 'n Slide. Behavior modification. Theirs or mine? Neither is working.

My goal now is to find indestructible furniture. Metal patio chairs. It could be a distinctive statement. When I'm tired of the industrial look of the grey metal, I could spray paint them all yellow and do a tropical theme.

With animal ownership, there is an inherent obligation to keep the house presentable. If you leave your seven-foot, Northern Pine artificial-Christmas-tree up year-round because the cats enjoy jumping in it, explain that. Make sure you tend to the kitty litter often. Otherwise, you'll be using air fresheners by the trunk load.

In addition, this now means that kitty litter is a major part of your budget. *Major.* You're buying the multiple cat stuff so it becomes a workout too when you buy it in 20-pound sacks. The price per ounce goes down exponentially when you shop at the warehouse store. You can pay about $2.50 for a gigantic 50-pound bag! Just try to pick it up. No problem, if you're in the habit of bench-pressing Buicks. I settle for those 20-pound buckets, and hope I don't lose my grip, drop it, and mutilate my foot.

Develop a sensitive nose to the kitty box odor. Some pet owners become oblivious to this. When your friends come to visit and bring portable respirators, you know things have gotten completely out of hand.

To make the kitty litter go farther, you scoop little deposits and flush them down the toilet. Then one day you read that flushing "used" kitty litter is endangering marine life! Evidently the kitty litter has harmful chemicals which may end up in the ocean. My friend, you're the direct cause of that whale beaching itself in Santa Monica!

So, you have made a commitment to the cat. Have you bonded with him? For better or for worse, 'til death do we part? Remember, above all else, this is an animal. It can have mysterious genealogy. Sweet, adorable, cuddly and the next moment he bites your nose off your face. Kitty therapy starts at about $100 an hour.

Earlier you probably laughed when I suggested a kitty trust fund, didn't you? Fast forward and you, with your kind heart, are spending hundreds, nay, thousands for Super Scoop, IAMS, catnip, play toys, vet bills, flea medication, insurance, therapy (for you and/or the cat) and new furniture. *You could have bought stock in Google.*

The same intense dedication and, dare I say, outrageous financial burden can apply to dogs. You feel sad because he's home alone all day, and he's no longer entertained by the *Dog Whisperer* reruns. You decide he needs friends. Doggie Day Care is next. Now, add the inevitable medical expenses and grooming because the dog looks sweet with those pink bows then, don't forget, the designer wardrobe.

There is a huge difference between cats and dogs. Cats stay home, and dogs come along. How often does your dog get to come with you? Is it teeny tiny so you carry it in a bag? Do you speak baby talk to it? How old are you? Is yours a big dog? One of those mean breeds? Intimidating breeds? How much liability insurance do you have?

There is a lot more! Does the dog slobber? Lick? Drool? If the new boyfriend is a clean freak, as in obsessive compulsive, you're in serious trouble. The first time the dog shakes his head and sprays the room with spit, your guy will be breaking the land-speed-record getting away from your house! As you can easily see, the pet thing can be troublesome.

Lastly, did you know that by carrying little dogs around they lose their concept of reality? They don't realize that they're supposed to be walking on the sidewalk. The elevated position allows them to assume the authority role and develop behavioral issues.

There is a big part of the population that does not want to deal with a dog or a cat. They love lizards or snakes, guinea pigs or ferrets and other creatures large, small and creepy. Plus, if they don't want a real pet in real life, they can always have it as an "App" which is way less expensive than anything else!

All of this gives me a headache. I think getting a screen saver with tropical fish swimming around would be much simpler.

COOKING

I'm sorry but cooking is so overrated. I have pots and pans. There are spider webs in them. My lack of enthusiasm shouldn't stop you from cooking, however. Inviting someone to your home to share in a yummy home-cooked meal is a great idea. Rachel Ray can guide you in her perky way to some *soup du jour* that will thrill your guests. My experience, on the other hand, has been disastrous. I have no sense for gathering ingredients, how much to gather, and how long anything should cook. I cook it too long or not long enough. That's where Cup O Noodles comes in. Meet me, Anita, the first person in the universe who screwed up Cup O Noodles.

My theory was to combine seven or eight Cup O Noodles to make a larger quantity. *Right?* My daughter's young grade-school friends were visiting, so why not make a noodle something. Kids love noodles anything.

I lined up eight containers, poured the boiling water in, gave each a quick stir and waited. After several minutes, I pulled off the lids and "poured" the containers' contents into the tureen. Each and every one of them plopped into the tureen. They were weird jelly blobs like alien amoebas exiting the little Styrofoam containers. Evidently after the boiling water is added, you are to *wait* several minutes before stirring. Now I had to "repair" the Cup O Noodles. I poured the concoction into a saucepan and simmered it into submission. It looked edible! I was feeding six-year-old kids. How discriminating could they be? They ate it all up like a ravenous pack of wolverines.

Despite my detour from the directions, I was pleased with the end result. The children were fed, and the cleanup was minimal!

Another close encounter with my culinary expertise was when I merely glanced at the instructions for bean soup. It was one of those self-contained, gourmet bags featuring four servings. I took the package and dumped the contents into a pot of boiling water. As the water simmered, the beans got larger. The pot was now overflowing. I had to transfer half the pot to another pot. *But it wasn't over yet.*

Three hours into the bean soup ordeal, I had transferred the contents two more times. I now had four huge pots happily bubbling away! I picked up the package and carefully looked at portions, servings, whatever. Where did I get this idea it served four? The recommendation was to measure the quantity you wished to prepare. The package contained enough for *four separate batches of soup if serving four.* I had gallons of bean soup. *Yes, it was gallons.* To this day, if I mention bean soup to my daughter, she runs screaming out the door!

There was a time when for Thanksgiving we would host 40 people at our house for dinner. My responsibility was to open the front door and welcome the guests. I was trusted with little else. My husband (at that time) was in charge of cooking as was my mother. They did an outstanding job. An overabundance of food was made each year. You could sit and eat until you exploded if you so chose. However, one year we ran out of mashed potatoes early into the dinner. *Very puzzling.* We didn't see guests packing potatoes into their pockets and purses so we assumed they were eaten early on.

About five days after that grand Thanksgiving event, I turned on the oven to bake some cupcakes with my daughter. After a few minutes, we smelled something odd. I peeked into the oven and discovered a huge pan of mashed potatoes. On Thanksgiving Day, it had been placed in the oven to stay warm but then it was forgotten.

This proved to me that I couldn't keep track of food once it was prepared for a dinner party. Also, I came to realize that an oven was wasted on me. My skill level was not even measurable! I am that person who doesn't use the oven enough to justify the space it occupies in one's home. Consequently, in my new home, I made the decision to do away with the wall oven. Instead, in its place, I have a beautiful saltwater aquarium.

I admit that anything I make needs to be foolproof and simple. Making something easy like a Tater Tot casserole builds my confidence. When I pull out the CorningWare to assemble this beautiful, gastronomical masterpiece, the children get excited. They smell it cooking, and they think I'm a god for having this kind of culinary talent.

"Mom, you're the best!" Here is an entrée that can deliver confidence, excitement, beauty and love. All that from a Tater Tot casserole! Fat grams being what they are, this delicious gem gets made once a year.

I confess that my friends know I can't cook. They rarely eat anything I prepare. As a result, they are all still alive and remain my friends! I consider that an achievement. To be absolutely truthful, there was a dinner years ago where my guests got food-poisoning. I rather not go into the details because I don't know if the statute of limitations has run out on that one.

There are times when you'll want to invite the boyfriend over for dinner and a movie. Still, I avoid making dinners. I prefer those that come knocking at the door and are handed to me in sturdy boxes from the fine dining establishments with multi-syllabic names like Dom-Mi-Nos Piz-e-Ria.

Kathy Griffin, the comedian, proudly serves up her Cake Soup to guests. Her recipe is not exactly revolutionary. In fact, you'll recognize it. What's important about it is that she gave it a name. It's (baked) cake mixed together with ice cream — any flavor cake, any flavor ice cream. What a lovely collaboration! The nutritional value of this concoction is highly questionable but, nonetheless, she's a genius!

I wanted to be a genius, too. I thought my opportunity had come when the local TV news happened to feature a segment, "How to Save Money by Making Your Own Microwave Popcorn." No need to purchase the expensive prepackaged kernels. *No.* All you need is regular, plain kernels and a medium-size paper bag. When they demonstrated it on TV, the news crew tasted it and raved about it. Cost per bag was mere pennies! This was for me. Save money? Sure, I'm on board.

Some friends were coming over one evening so I figured this was the perfect time to show them my new technique for microwave popcorn. I invited them into the kitchen. I poured the popcorn into the bag, put the bag into the microwave, set the timer, and stood back.

I then bragged about how much money I was saving by not buying the prepackaged bags. *Ingenious!*

We were all standing around, staring at the bag in the microwave. It spun around several times on the little turn table, the bag puffed up and then burst into flames! I grabbed my designer fire extinguisher and sprang into action. I opened the microwave and quelled the raging inferno. Things were again under control. My friends were impressed with my heroic action. We called for a pizza.

My friends do not think it's a good idea for me to attend cooking school for fear I will burn down the place. As you have seen, they could be right!

If you want to improve your culinary skills, they have plenty of cooking shows on TV. *Bitchin' Kitchen* is my style. *It's crazy.* It is pretty simple to follow and outrageously entertaining. I will admit to watching *Top Chef* but was stunned when a contestant mentioned using 27 ingredients for his dish. I use four ingredients when I make spaghetti: spaghetti noodles, Prego, salt, pepper. I think 27 ingredients is overkill.

Before leaving the subject of cooking, a poster of the Heimlich maneuver is proudly displayed in my kitchen. I believe no home should be without one.

GUESTS

How do out-of-town guests work into this? *Easy.* They introduce *the unknown.* These guests are the people who can add immense pleasure and adventure to your life. They come from a different part of the country or world. They have had totally unique experiences.

This doesn't mean you have to have a place large enough to accommodate them. The nearby Hyatt is fine. Be available for whatever they want to do. Theme parks, museums, even a shopping mall can be delightful because your guests will often invite "old" friends from the area to accompany them. It may turn out to be someone of immeasurable merit who happens to be an engaging conversationalist and more.

If you're currently dating someone, having him meet these individuals could be intimidating or awkward. Don't allow too many questions. That makes anyone nervous. Keep it superficial. Keep it safe!

A close friend of mine was dating a young man who was from a very conservative family. Think Amish. and you're pretty close to their lifestyle. Maryanne had never met his parents but the time had come. She invited them for dinner along with a few of her own family members. She was dreading it. There was a questionable past that could come up. It wasn't hers. It was her grandmother's! During dinner her sister started to talk about their beloved Nanah Naomi.

117

Nanah Naomi was a very sweet, unassuming woman. Her face was angelic – light blue eyes and rosy pink cheeks. She lived a very simple life. She often sat on the front porch with the grandchildren and neighborhood kids who were there for her story time. The next one was always better than the last. What a vivid imagination because she never ran out of the *alleged* escapades.

When she passed away, Maryanne's father inherited her house. There were no large bank accounts. No jewelry to speak of. But her father suspected money was hidden in that house somewhere. He began disassembling it. Within a month or two, there was a big pile of building material where the house once stood. He had found money hidden everywhere–the radiators, glued in with the wallpaper, under the linoleum. He had found thousands and thousands of dollars! But he wasn't finished yet.

Nanah Naomi always gave the children money from a coffee can. Where were they? Buried in the yard? Maryanne's father brought in metal detectors and found dozens of coffee cans filled with cash that had been interred on the property.

The dinner guests asked almost in unison, "Where did all the money come from?"

Maryanne's sister responded excitedly, "Wow! That's the crazy part! My dad let us in on the secret. During Prohibition she was known as a dare devil. She was a gun runner! Nanah made big money doing that and by driving "hootch," you know "booze," to speakeasies! Isn't that cool?"

I have interesting and quirky cousins who visit me every so often. They have a wacky hobby. They travel the world with the mission of visiting family graves and checking out the headstones. I would find musical theater more satisfying; but when they make their reservations for Tahiti to check for graves, I plan to go along.

When friends or family visit, they usually get snoopy wanting to know who you're dating. *How is your life going? Are you serious with anyone?* That's when they offer you those sweet catch phrases: *Be true to yourself. Only the strong survive.* This psycho-babble makes me want to tear my hair out. How about you? But then as a "thank you" for your hospitality, they give you a stupid refrigerator magnet with another philosophical nugget of nonsense.

As you pass through the kitchen, catching a glimpse of such a phrase could inspire you, encourage you, and improve your loser thought-process. *Nah.* The magnets are evidence. Unknowingly, you're exposing a weak spot. You invite a guy over to visit and totally forget that on your refrigerator is a year's worth of Dr. Phil homilies. Believe me, your unsuspecting male friend, upon seeing this refrigerator door/therapeutic message wall, will wonder how long you've been in therapy and how many more years you have to go!

Take the magnets. Put them in a drawer. If you have too many of them to even fit into a drawer, throw some away. Don't stop to argue with yourself as to which ones to keep. Be brave. Take a handful, close your eyes and put them in the Goodwill bag. The magnets will go on to benefit another needy soul somewhere in this great land of ours!

Sometimes you will have guests whose visits become quite the event. Chances are that you will be the recipient of memories that come once in a lifetime and new relationships that may last just as long! This was the case when I would host a visiting minister. He was well known to my daughter, Christina, and stepped in as a grandpa figure. His name was Kermit. Unusual name since the only Kermit we were familiar with at that time was a frog with a TV show.

One afternoon our house guest was paid a visit by two young seminary students. I judged them to be about my age … thirty or so at that time. I couldn't help but consider what they had chosen as their life path, and what I had chosen as mine. Their goal was to focus on theology and the study of God's Word. On the other hand, there was me. My focus at that particular time in my life was to learn how to tap dance.

I directed them to the guest house where Kermit was staying. One young man turned to ask if I had an extra Bible. I told him I would have my young daughter run one back to them.

Christina, who was four, was sitting on the patio. I handed her the Bible and asked her to take it to Kermit. She jumped off her chair and disappeared around the corner of the porch. Fifteen minutes later, the young man poked his head in the door and asked about the Bible.

Surprised, I responded that I had given it to Christina to deliver. Maybe she had gotten distracted? I peeked into her room, and saw that she was playing with several of her dolls. They were all sitting on the floor in a circle enjoying a tea party. There, sitting right between Raggedy Ann and Minnie Mouse was Kermit the Frog with the Bible on his lap.

A LIFE-SIZE, BLACK & WHITE COW

I believe in conversation pieces. "You" can be the conversation piece or something you own can be a conversation piece. He needs to be able to remember you. It's all part of the theory that your reputation should precede you. *"Did you see Tony's Picasso?" "How about Leanne's toothpick display?"*

Folks have magnificent collections of ceramic frogs or fairies. Usually, they are souvenirs from trips to Niagara Falls, Peoria or simply another proud purchase from QVC. Nice tidy stuff that lives inside the house which requires dusting and upkeep. I don't believe in that. My conversation piece is a magnificent, full-size, black-and-white fiberglass cow who lives in my backyard. Her name is Lucy. She became a member of the family due to another one of my complete moments of insanity.

It began as a normal Saturday morning. I stood on the back porch with my cup of coffee calmly looking around the yard. I will blame it on the caffeine kicking in because suddenly I recognized how dull the yard was. *It was pathetic.* Nicely landscaped, I suppose, but there was no getting around it. The yard was boring. It needed something large and impressive. That's when it occurred to me. A cow would make the difference.

I checked the Internet and found someone who specialized in fiberglass animals. "Chuck" had a good selection and had been around since the 1970s. I phoned him immediately. Did he have a cow? A full-size cow? Not only did he have a cow, he had horses, chickens, rabbits and ponies! *This was my guy!* So I asked him, "Where are you?" "Can I buy a cow to go?" and "Could I come right now?"

It didn't matter to me that he was more than a 100 miles away. When I told my friend, Rich, about my road trip, he was horrified. "What if this guy is a weird tobacco-chewing maniac who lives in a shack, sits on his front porch in a rocking chair, and plays a banjo out there? You could get killed! You'll become a storyline on *CSI*!"

Rich insisted upon coming along to protect me. He didn't bring a gun or baseball bat, though. I guess my can of hair spray on the back seat of the car could have served as a weapon if it had come to that.

We drove out of the city. The stands of trees were replaced by cactus and tumbleweeds as we ascended into the high desert. No road trip is complete without singing along to Elvis so we did enjoy ourselves during this drive. I think we were especially lively on "Suspicious Minds."

Desolate was pretty much the description that crossed my mind as we turned onto the designated street. As we slowed down to check addresses, we both were stunned by our discovery. We exclaimed in unison, "Can you believe this?"

We pulled up to our destination. It was a veritable fiberglass animal nirvana. Dozens of pigs, a row of ponies, two stallions rearing up on their back legs, cows with calves, roosters, chickens and so much more!

There was no shack. It was nice, expansive stucco. No scary tobacco-chewing man sat on the front porch in a rocking chair playing a banjo. A good-looking, fortyish man came out of the front door to greet us. I assumed this was our contact, "Chuck." We walked from the car toward the house, and I recognized that Chuck had an amazing resemblance to (I had to pause for a breath) Brad Pitt! What was a guy like this doing in the middle of nowhere? And why wasn't I dating him? He was totally a geographic undesirable! *What a shame!*

I introduced myself to him. I made sure I introduced Rich as *my friend*. I didn't want this lovely creature to assume "we" were married. The three of us talked for an hour as Chuck gave us a tour of his "farm." He was a sweet, gentle soul. He had gotten tired of Los Angeles, and he wanted a simpler life. He moved out to the desert quite some time ago. He made his animals, enjoyed the quiet nature of his efforts, and took great pleasure in finding his animals new homes.

I fell in love with him right then and there. How could I not buy a cow from this spiritual person? I didn't even talk him down on the price. I probably paid way too much, but I'm not used to negotiating the purchase of a life-size cow, for heaven's sake! We strapped it on top of my car and drove back to Pasadena.

Rich, exceptional artist that he is, designed and painted on her black spots. They brought her to life. The *au couture* outfit she wears was his idea too. She proudly sports a hat, shawl, sunglasses, and glittery pink roller-skates.

Lucy joined the two other animals in the yard: our beloved, four-foot baby elephant named "Ralph" and our lanky, eight-foot dinosaur named "Daisy." It's nice to be identified with something unique and special.

There are those people in our world who are devoid of the silly heart complex. To them, acquiring and enjoying full-size, fiberglass animals is stupid. My guess is that they're just jealous. They probably don't even have a garden gnome.

I do.

HIS "HOME SWEET HOME"

Where does he live? By getting his address, you can google it to see the street view of the property. Is the apartment building surrounded by razor wire? A big house would be swell but that could translate into seven roommates. Does he rent or own? Don't overlook the possibility that he may be sleeping on his best friend's couch. What if he's still living with his parents? That's no big deal as long as he's occupying the quaint carriage house on the family's four-acre estate.

If he invites you to visit his home sweet home, you absolutely must! By visiting, you can check whether he has a bobble head collection or if he's a hoarder. Hidden from view might be women's clothing in a closet. Do they belong to another one of his girlfriends or could they be his? Are all of the shirts he owns plaid? Does he have parties and make beer in his bathtub?

A few well-directed questions, and you can determine what his status is. Luxury homes can be rented. Luxury cars can be leased.

Watch out for the fibbers. Don't be shocked if you find out that his total worth is equal to the price of a one topping pizza. Mr. Liar Liar Pants on Fire will try to romance you. When you realize it's all smoke and mirrors, put on your respirator and goggles, then get out of there.

$\mathcal{G}$AINFULLY EMPLOYED

EMPLOYMENT

Soon after meeting him, you'll surely ask, *"What business are you in?"* Be aware that you can be too quick to dismiss him if you aren't careful. Do you only want someone who works in an Armani suit? What if he only wears shorts for his job? Will that scare you off? Well, think again. His name could be David Beckham. Afraid that he might be a circus performer? You should be so lucky if he works for Cirque du Soleil. (Hint: You could install a trapeze in the bedroom.) You're on your own if he admits to being a mail-order herring merchant or an apprentice plate spinner.

Believing what they claim to do is a challenge. I don't know where you live but Los Angeles is full of fibbers. Rely on your experience and what is plausible. You may notice a new group of guys in the club. They smile at you, walk over your way, and introduce themselves to you and your friends. You find them to be polite, well-spoken, good-looking and physically fit. You ask if they're visiting LA as tourists or in town to perform?

One member of the group replies that they're on tour. Cool! They're probably in a band or something. Nope, they are all cage fighters! Cage fighters? What kind of a world are we living in? I was not prepared for this answer at all.

In these days of massive unemployment, so many people are looking for jobs. When I got laid off, I was devastated. I began applying for anything. I have stellar credentials as a Communications Specialist, Video Producer and a Circus Clown. If anything, I'm diversified.

When I visited the local pet store, I noticed the posting for a position as a Doggie Day Camp Associate. This job puts you in the huge, floor-to-ceiling glass-walled dog house which occupies the entire back of the store. It's a temperature-controlled environment so all those being held captive are comfortable. The critters, large and small, visit and play together. It's like a huge aquarium for dogs sans water!

Your job is to keep the pups happy and safe. Some of these dogs are huge! Keep in mind that you have to be brave enough to put yourself in the middle of snarling teeth to break up the bad boys. But, be assured, each "canine camper" is investigated and profiled. They make sure "Killer" is a social sort and hasn't ripped someone's head off in the recent past.

I filled out the 19-page application. Yes, 19 pages! The personality profile had all of those trick questions (where they take one issue and reword it five different ways). For instance: "Do you tend to be a patient person?" "Are you patient with rude customers?" "Do rude customers upset you?" Personally, I would be more inclined to shoot rude customers but that option wasn't given.

I didn't get the job. I still don't know why. I followed up but they probably thought I was overqualified. I think they passed up on hiring someone who could have been one of their premier employees. They could have taken advantage of my literary background and allowed me to read Shakespeare to the dogs. Then with my experience as a circus clown, I would have taught the dogs to jump through hoops. It's clear to me. Those Human Resource people are not visionaries.

ENTREPRENEUR

What unique ability or talent do you have? What can people pay you to do or what product or service could you sell them? Guys appreciate a female who has her own business. In fact, I had a company called Rent-a-Groupie. It was the ultimate meet-and-greet service — a uniquely LA thing to do. When a company's top sales-people would be sent to Los Angeles, Rent-a-Groupie would meet that person at the airport. This was all before 9/11 so life could be more spontaneous and fun.

A dozen male and female employees that were from Rent-a-Groupie would be at the gate, autograph books in hand, screaming as though this person was a hugely popular celebrity. "Photographers" were there to create the paparazzi frenzy all while the other passengers in the terminal guessed amongst themselves, "Who is he? Do you recognize him?" We pulled this off dozens of times. It was silly and outrageous. Now we could branch out into Rent-a-Paparazzi!

As a matter of fact, someone at Disney heard about my company and contacted me about a job in promotions. I would travel the country with the Disney characters. These are the actors Disney hires to appear as Mickey, Minnie, Donald and the others! *Fun!* Essentially, I would be their keeper for special events as well as the on-location producer. *Party on!* The magic wore off when the true logistics were broken down. Because of the value of the trademarked Disney character suits, some items would have to be hand-carried at all times. Yes, I would have to carry Mickey's head around in a box. Instead, I went on to become a circus clown.

Being an entrepreneur brings with it tremendous responsibilities. Working 24/7, constant travel, astute business sense, and taking risks. If he is an entrepreneur, you could be enjoying a lovely dinner with him only to be interrupted by a phone call notifying him that the Chief Financial Officer just took off with all the company's money. Be supportive and find out where the scoundrel went so both of you can join him!

$\mathcal{L}$OOKS & PERSONAL STUFF

LOOKS

Have you been hydrating? Using anti-aging cream? For how long? Was I supposed to start hydrating when I was 10? How's it going for you? When you look in the mirror, are you frightened? I am.

AGE

What a joke! It doesn't matter how old you are when you're out there dating. You could be 20, and he is 60. You could look 60, and he could look 20. How old do you look? How old you feel? *Blah Blah Blah.*

You can buy a pretty face and Brazilian butt. Liposuction that chin and neck. Get cheek implants for definition. Go into debt for a dazzling smile with veneers. Remove some ribs to trim that middle. You

133

don't have to look like you if you don't want to any longer! Unfortunately, I can't afford all of these procedures but I need to do them all. I think I'll have a telethon.

This is why time is of the essence. The longer I wait the longer the list gets, and the more expensive it becomes! I must remain optimistic. I'm waiting for coupons. Anything to cut down the initial expense of a full-blown makeover. I do foresee the day when we have low-cost Drive-Thru Liposuction. It will be a nationwide franchise, and they'll offer coupons plus Wednesday afternoon specials. I'm getting excited already!

PASSAGE OF TIME

Congratulations if you're one of those people who only gets better looking as you get older. This will come in handy when you're dating or just moving along through your life. Now, go ahead, admit that you're an alien from outer space.

Are you that breathtakingly handsome guy or stunningly beautiful woman who has never known anything else in your life except being good looking? You've lived your life not knowing anything different? Well, as I see it, you're monopolizing every last bit of beauty karma from our world, and I'm out here suffering with way too little..

A celebrity, finally, shared her *secret* to looking so beautiful. It was Heather Locklear. She looks magnificent and continues to look splendid decade after decade. She absolutely does *not* suffer from the ravages of time. Anyway, Heather claims it's due to sleeping on her back.

When I sleep, I'm one of those people who tosses and turns. I become a contortionist while I sleep. I can start out on my back but end up on my right side, my right arm is twisted underneath me, and it's completely numb. Still, Heather's tip is worth trying. So, to keep myself on my back during sleepy time, I will purchase bungee cords and will strap myself into place.

BEAUTY

Beauty is only skin deep. Who came up with that? I bet someone ugly.

Before beginning your process for perfection, look in the mirror and smile. Realize your potential and value. Then start putting on your makeup and doing your hair. Check yourself from head to toe before exiting the bathroom an hour and a half later. Without missing a beat, one of your kids will ask, "Are you ready for your date? Hey, what's with your hair?"

As for beauty, I only see a nip and a tuck as being able to help me at this point. When I was growing up, we landed on the Moon. OK, so we got them on the Moon. Now, on to more important things. Wasn't anyone thinking about those of us who would get saggy and wrinkly? Technology is supposed to help us. This should have been a government funded program — a lotion, a cream, something that would keep us looking young and stunning. Something that would be *so* revolutionary, it would tear a hole in the fabric of time. It would be manufactured by our government, and sold by the Feds with the money benefiting our general fund. No dollars going overseas. *It stays right here! The country would be flush with cash! Billions and billions of dollars would be rolling in!* I am a taxpayer. I deserve our country's and technology's best efforts. *Why hasn't anybody thought of this before?*

It's always commendable when we try to save money on cosmetics and beauty treatments. Hair cuts, coloring and perms can be very pricey. Several years ago, I decided that my hair needed a nice body perm but I didn't want to visit a salon and pay $100 plus tip. Perm kits are sold at Target. They're only $15. I decided I would do my hair myself. *How hard can it be, really?* When I mentioned my plan to my friend, Rich, he offered to help. After all, when he was a little boy, he helped his mom when she did home perms. He was an experienced hair do-er!

I gathered the items required and prepared the kitchen for our evening of beauty. We carefully read the directions and started the process. My hair was sectioned off and ready for the transformation. Rich made his way around my head. He carefully installed the pink rollers until every strand had been captured. Next, we poured the stinky potion onto my head. We properly saturated my hair. We sat down to relax and let the time pass until the final rinse. I reached up to pat my head and made a terrifying discovery. Rich had rolled my hair into the wrong direction! The top was going forward. The sides were rolled up. The back went up. My hair was going to look like the Bride of Frankenstein!

I ran to the bathroom mirror to confirm what I suspected. I ran back to the kitchen and put my head under the faucet. Rich and I pulled out the rollers while I tried to rinse the perm out of my hair! The damage was not serious. For four weeks, my hair looked curly and confused. Interesting yet odd. I've stayed away from perms from that day on. That was Rich's last perm, too. He went on to become an award-winning Creative Director of a big corporation. His comments now about my hair are limited to: your hair looks fantastic or oh, my God, I hope you brought your hat!

Beauty and Gravity. Gravity is no one's friend. They now want us to use anti-gravity machines to stay young-looking. Fifteen minutes a day hanging upside down will get that blood flowing better. I think it is pointless. I was strapped into one of those contraptions and was terrified. What if the person who strapped me in gets a phone call, forgets about me and leaves? What happens if there is an earthquake? If I sneeze, will my head explode from all the extra blood in it? The trainer then suggested the program would involve my hanging upside down and reaching/bending upwards from my waist to touch my toes. I can't stand on solid ground and bend down to touch my toes. I resigned from the class.

Beauty and the Nighttime Humidifier Treatment. I have a friend with a complexion that is flawless. It's almost like porcelain. Well, she credits her fantastic skin to sleeping with a cool-mist humidifier humming away all night long. She has done this for years, and she's gorgeous. Her skin positively glows. This could be an inexpensive solution for me! My skin needed nourishment, and this Nighttime Humidifier Beauty Treatment was effortless! The transformation to beauty occurs while I'm *sleeping*. I could not wait to get started!

I immediately purchased my very own cool-mist unit. That evening it took an hour of tweaking to get the humidifier to circulate the proper amount of water and turn it into a velvety mist. In days, the plants in my room were flourishing! The clothes in my closet no longer needed ironing! My skin? I don't know. Too soon to tell.

After a month, my bedroom was bordering on swampish. I did not want to give up. To enhance the environment, I added more ferns, orchids and hanging moss. I installed special effect lighting– fiber optic fire flies! I don't think I overlooked anything!

Late one evening my daughter stood at the doorway and looked around. "Mom, I think you have gotten carried away with this humidifier thing. Your bedroom looks like the "Pirates of the Caribbean!" ride!"

I realized something WAS missing! I dashed to the computer and ordered the life size standup of "Captain Jack Sparrow!" Every night while my skin is being revitalized, I'll be sleeping with Johnny Depp!

MINIMUM THRESHOLD OF ATTRACTIVENESS

Sometimes do you think that you have already peaked? When? *Yesterday? Last week? Last year?* It all comes down to how much of an effort you are making. Are you even making an effort? If you have committed yourself to the full regimen, you will have clean elbows. Check them. Check your boyfriend's. You will be shocked to hear that more then 50 percent of people walking among us have dirty elbows. Well, did you check yours?

A quick note about teeth, though. "He has his own teeth" means nothing anymore. Nobody has their own teeth. In Los Angeles, you don't want to have your own teeth. You want caps, crowns and veneers so you'll have a dazzling smile. If he has a dazzling smile, it could mean he passed up owning an E-Class Mercedes to get that pretty. Pretty does have its price.

I've done the at-home whitening strips. I've swallowed at least a half dozen of them. I think my teeth are whiter but I got concerned when warned about the problems that can result with the whitening. Sensitivity can occur that can destroy your ability to comfortably eat ice cream and even drink cold beverages like a perfectly blended martini. I stopped whitening immediately. I couldn't take that risk!

FACIAL PUNCTUATION

Make sure your face can communicate how you feel. You don't have to talk all of the time, for Pete's sake. If something is annoying, roll your eyes. If something is exciting, inhale slightly and open your eyes really wide. *Smile.*

I'm sure you have an idea of how to look sad. Most people are at a loss if they need to show real emotion: disgust, excitement, even love! The flair for the dramatic is a natural gift for some and learned behavior for others. Reason enough why improv classes and theater should be mandatory in high school.

Practice in front of the mirror and get these things down. If you have a face full of Botox, you'll probably have to push your face into the appropriate positions. Too many more of those injections, and your future face flexibility will be seriously compromised.

HANDS AND FEET

While I was growing up, I learned about the essential items to make myself more attractive. Lovely, clean fingernails are part of that regimen. Nail polish, nail strengthener polish or the go-to Lee Press-On Nails and there's a lot more. The Lee nails are still around today because this product is a profound contribution to our civilization. I have worn them with pride. But most of the time, I go *au natural.*

I have short fingers and less than exciting fingernails. I can't recall a guy holding my hand and commenting about my fingernails. When it comes to manicures, there's an investment to be made as well. Standard manicures with polish can be under $50. If you want acrylic nails and all of the special stuff, you can be spending $100 to $200. Then he doesn't even notice them?

How does anyone with those long nails remove their contact lenses? I am always waiting for an eyeball to go shooting across the table when one of my friends "adjusts" her lenses. *It's scary.* Furthermore, fingernails and the nails you put on your fingernails (isn't this redundant?) are not cheap. Did you want tips with acrylic overlay, standard acrylic overlay, forever French acrylic, standard fill-in, acrylic fill-in, nail art, basic manicure, French or American manicure? How about little flowers painted on those nails or little symbols for Christmas, New Year's Eve or candles for your birthday? *Can't we have clean fingernails and call it a day?*

Don't question the necessity of a pedicure. Even when you think you're being thrifty by chewing off your own toe nails. No, it is not entertaining when you demonstrate that you can get your foot up to your mouth. *Knock it off.* The other important reason for a pedicure is for the moment when you curl up on his couch. He invites you to take your boots off.

You reply, "I already did."

He glances over again, and realizes that he's looking at the soles of your feet! Does tire tread come to mind? Schedule pedicures on your calendar! *No! Better yet.* Each day, LOOK at your feet, make an evaluation: *pretty, acceptable, hideous?*

As for him? Does he have big feet? Little feet? Stinking feet? Feet like a hobbit? Hairy? When you are concerned about what you can *get* from someone, don't forget what his feet could have. Caution is the word with athlete's foot, ring worm … then he may have a garden-variety fungus depositing itself in your shower when he stays overnight.

Guys have barely presentable feet. A description? *Downright putrid.* I have seen guys who wear gigantic size-12 sandals frighten small children! The huge, yellow toe nails, hair on the top of their feet and on their toes are too shocking for impressionable youngsters.

Anyway, how are his nails? Does he trim them with a nail clipper? This is such a deal-breaker. Where does he clip? Where does he deposit the clipped bits? When the clipping is done in public, someone sitting nearby is in danger of losing an eyeball because of an errant fingernail hurtling through space right into their cornea. Those clipped bits when they take flight are going at least 25 miles per hour! Are the nail bits thrown to the floor so if you walk barefoot his nail bits can stick to your feet? I think I have communicated the point.

No, there's actually more. I have a friend whose boyfriend clips his toenails in the shower. When she takes a bath, his toenail bits that did not go down the drain (he makes no effort to make sure they do) end up floating around her in the tub. How icky is that? See how things like this can be a disgusting visual, even when it's not happening to you personally?

EYELASHES

Do they curl? Dark enough? Thick enough? As if there isn't enough to worry about, we have to stress out over our eyelashes. Get big, fat, fake ones! You can get inexpensive ones at Wal-Mart or have the salon install them for several hundred dollars.

If you decide to plaster those big, fat fake two-inch eyelashes onto your lids, *be* careful. Eyelashes can fall off, land in your drink, and float around like a dead caterpillar. This happened to Connie, a friend of mine,

143

while sitting across from Mr. Holy Cow is He a Doll on their first date. She could feel the eyelash peeling from her eyelid. With the next blink, she realized the eyelash was slowly disengaging itself. Should she pull it off? Maybe it would stop halfway. No such luck. The eyelash sprang from the lid and sailed right into her drink.

Her date grabbed her glass. "Don't drink that," he warned. "There's a bug in it!"

He started laughing when he recognized what was in the glass and then looked at her very naked left eye. She, with a smile, peeled off the other eyelash and placed in on the table. "I give up."

Of course, you may feel the eyelash issue is important enough to go through an evaluation by a doctor and have medication prescribed to grow your eyelashes to a longer length! I don't think you should do this if your boyfriend is staying overnight. You could apply this medication and wake up with eyelashes so outrageously long they would need to be braided! Your boyfriend would think you've turned into something from a horror movie.

REJUVENATE & REPLENISH

How can we possibly be well versed in politics and current events when we have no time? We make an appointment at a spa or salon, and then need to spend 10 minutes of our valuable time reviewing the spa menu. We need to evaluate what our body is screaming for … then know what to request! We then add up the bill and go into cardiac arrest. Deep cleansing, aromatherapy, pumpkin peel, sensitive skin facial, radiance facial, deep tissue massage, Swedish, reflexology, neuromuscular, hot stone. God forbid that you're hairy. Take a shot of tequila and go get waxed. Full leg, half leg, bikini, Brazilian, underarm, eyebrow, lip, chin and ears.

You can't leave the salon looking pasty white if you're a *Caucasian du jour.* Step into the booth for a spray-on tan.

Body sculpting. I could eat air and get fat. I need special services. Maybe you are one of those people as well. I call it "high maintenance" or "thigh maintenance." I don't really know if those deep, intense massages do anything other than make the salon a lot of money. I am hopeful a half an inch may have been pushed into another location.

Some people swear by these massages and claim they're relaxing. I feel like I'm being beaten to death and subsequently ache for the next two weeks. The suffering is just part of the effort to pound the cellulite into submission. In my case, the salon has been using a jackhammer and the estimate for completion is about a year.

This is an option to consider if you need to lose a few pounds or inches in 60 minutes … just trot down to the salon. Get one of those full body wraps that brings

you down a size or two temporarily. They force all moisture out of your body. Of course, when you drink some
water, you'll burst out of your dress. Hopefully that is
after the event, and he has left the building.

DIETS

Be cautious about going on diets to slim down for your
dating life. The Snow Cone Diet and that Cracker-a-
Day Diet can catch up with you. Taking drugs to lose
weight can be mighty risky. Recently another prescription diet medication was taken off the market because
of a serious side effect — liver failure. The other more
serious side effect was death. People were dropping
like flies!

You don't want to be a casualty of something as
hideous as a prescription diet pill. You could be on a
first date having dinner with some terrific guy and have
your spleen explode! That could really screw up your
chances for a second date.

HERBS AND SUPPLEMENTS

One good thing about dating these days is that, by and
large, the majority of the population does its best to stay

healthy. We are convinced that flinging some unpronounceable herbs down our throats every day is beneficial. We will then age gracefully. Maybe because we ate all of those herbs, we would remember our names when we are 90.

We place so much trust in the vitamins and dietary supplements that we take. Some people take hundreds of pills a day. Suzanne Somers looks fantastic, and she credits it to her daily consumption of dozens of vitamins, supplements, and so on. I can't even remember to take my One-A-Day.

Do you worry about your brain? Tumors, aneurysms, cancer and plenty of other wretched diseases can befall you. I constantly have a circus in my brain but, I confess, I enjoy it.

As for keeping our brains healthy, we were encouraged take ginkgo biloba. It's been a popular herbal supplement for about two decades. Recently it underwent another comprehensive study. After a year of research, ginkgo biloba didn't prevent dementia or Alzheimer's disease in participants. There wasn't any evidence that the herb reduced the cognitive decline that is associated with aging.

I was disappointed. I think I spent a lot of money on ginkgo biloba. I can't remember.

COSMETICS

While clothes shopping for that special date, did anything seem different to you in the department stores? Have you noticed that the expensive makeup, wrinkle removers and skin regimens are now being kept behind lock and key? This is like the expensive liquor at the grocery store. It makes for an interesting comparison. You can either buy the pricey cosmetics which may or may not work. Or you could buy the pricey alcohol, drink enough of it and not worry about how you look.

Does your date wear makeup? At first, this question seems odd, but look at Steven Tyler and Dave Navarro. Cosmetics work for them! Foundation, powder, blush, mascara, eyeliner, concealer, eyebrow pencil and lipstick could bring you together. You can apply makeup on each other to find that perfect face.

Don't dismiss this idea so quickly. Remember how hard it is to pencil on your eyebrows? The left side never matches the right. Now someone can help you determine the ideal arch for your face, the length of the brow, and width. You would have your own personal makeup artist! Life has never been better. I suppose he will have a flaw somewhere. Whatever it is. Overlook it!

Since I haven't yet found my very own personal makeup artist, my solution for the eyebrow issue is to leave one side of my bangs a little longer, then let the hair gently fall over that eyebrow. Perfect camouflage. I have already decided that when my eyelids get droopy, I'll do much the same ... I will let my hair grow down into my eyes. I'll eventually look like Cousin It from *The Addams Family*. I won't feel offended if you copy my idea.

Cosmetics now can be airbrushed on, you know. You fill up the gallon tank with foundation, hook up the sprayer and beauty is layered on until you achieve a level of satisfaction. Don't scratch your cheek as a crevice or canyon could appear. Don't show any expression or your face may crack.

The greatest part of the airbrush cosmetics are the fillers that can be used underneath. Putty for those wrinkles gets smoothed out and becomes indistinguishable under the application of spray-on goop. *Watch out ...* your face is now untouchable. And don't get too warm or your face could slide off onto his shirt. Those kinds of situations are so difficult to explain away.

BEAUTY SECRETS

An interesting recommendation is that to stay looking younger for your love life, live in a cold climate. I can't live in a cold climate because I live in Southern California. Cold in Southern California is 60 degrees. I think they're talking about colder than that. Anyway, I am following their advice to stay wrinkle-free and doing the best that I can using what I have at my disposal. I spend at least five minutes a day with my face in the freezer. I think it's working.

Also, I recently read about the beneficial properties of cucumbers. Why there hasn't been a run on them is beyond my comprehension. If this procedure works, the price for a pound of cucumbers will equal that of gold! The whole idea is not to eat them but to rub them on your cellulite! Cellulite is hideous, and it has been judged to be a crime against humanity.

Here's what's involved. Slice up the cucumber. Rub the cucumber pieces on the problem areas. Do this for a few minutes. You'll find the phytochemicals in the cucumber causes the collagen in your skin to tighten, firming up the outer layer and reducing the visibility of cellulite. If you have a small amount of cellulite (lucky you), a cucumber or two might suffice. You might need to buy several dozen if you're loaded with cellulite.

The article didn't indicate how many times a day or week you need to do this. Nor did it give any information as to how long it reduces the visibility of cellulite.

I'm on my way to the grocery store right this minute to purchase cucumbers. I will be renting a skip loader to get them delivered to my house. I think I need a hundred pounds or more.

JEWELRY

Will your dates find your jewelry tasteful? Are you wearing locomotive parts as jewelry? Do *you* think it's tasteful? "Kind of" is not an answer. Do you think you can fool someone into believing those fourteen-carat synthetic diamonds on your hands or ears are real? If you can't afford real, don't wear fake. It's so easy to be tacky.

Hopefully, your bracelets don't jangle like wind chimes. Crucial to this, as well, are earrings. I see some women wearing what looks like shower curtain rings in their ears. If they are hoops, are they big enough for an Olympic gymnast to use for an exercise routine? *If so, get rid of them.* Hoop or dangle, they should not hang from your ear lobe and be resting on your shoulder. We don't want Prince Charming to get caught in them. This could lead to an unfortunate incident necessitating a call to 911. *Use your imagination.*

You can easily disfigure yourself by wearing heavy, dangling earrings. They can damage the ear lobe by stretching it and tearing it. Ear-lobe cosmetic surgery is becoming quite popular. The doctors are repairing the careless accessorizing which both men and women are guilty of committing. When earrings you insist upon wearing weigh as much as cinder blocks, it's a good bet your ear lobe will suffer.

I believe, thank God, we have seen the last of the puka shell necklaces. *Or just about.* Every so often, you might spot one on *The Jerry Springer Show*. Chances are you won't be bumping into Mr. Puka Shell at the opera so you're safe. Be wary though of his commitment to gold ... necklaces, chains, crosses. If he's wearing one of those gold medallions that are the size of a Volkswagen, you need to go running into the sunset. *Alone!*

If his bling clangs together, this is another danger sign. If you're dancing with him, this jangle of precious metal could become a deadly weapon, smacking you in the head. Pretty pathetic when you receive a concussion from your boyfriend's jewelry.

Gold teeth? *I have no comment.*

HANDBAGS

Purse? Handbag? Fanny pack? If you need to make a fashion statement with your handbag, *be careful.* One, think expensive. The price of a designer bag is the same as a two-bedroom stucco in Wichita. Second, the size of these handbags is crazy. They look like a feedbag for a horse. Without anything inside the bags, they weigh in at 10 pounds. They're usually adorned with heavy chains and medallions. Put in your phone, wallet, water bottle, makeup, hair product, and Altoids. Your handbag weighs 20 pounds. That's considerably heavier than a portable defibrillator!

Designer bags make such an important statement that women will buy counterfeit ones or seconds from outlet shops. A grand and glorious designer handbag will forgive you of any horrible fashion mistake. If you have cutoff jeans and are carrying a Judith Lieber beaded bag, people might bow and curtsy in your presence.

Be careful about hanging your purse on the back of your chair. If you go out for dinner, your purse might be heavier than the chair. If you get up, the chair could flip over with the weight of your bag. *Place it on the floor.* Make sure that the serving staff won't be tripping over it. At the end of dinner, if your date leans over to pick up the purse, warn him about the weight. He could feel a twinge of pain as he lifts it. You have given him a hernia. Don't be surprised if the next time you see him is in court with Larry Parker for a personal injury lawsuit. It's all your fault for toting around a bag that could double as a Mini Cooper if you put wheels on it.

Further, an assault charge can manifest itself when you lug that purse on your shoulder, walk through a crowded area, inadvertently push up against someone and break their ribs. Then consider what the sheer weight of this bag could be doing to you physically. I have had a heavy shoulder-bag drop down onto my forearm and bruise my left arm. I would switch shoulders and have the same thing happen to the right arm. Bruises from my wrists to my elbows. *It was pathetic.* By looking at my arms, you would assume that I had been participating in *Saturday Night SmackDown.*

Don't forget as you insist upon hanging a gigantic bag on your shoulder, you will eventually start to bend over from the weight. A rounded hunch could develop. Nice if you're dating the Hunchback of Notre Dame. You will make a cute couple.

There's a benefit to carrying a large purse. If it's really gigantic, it can make you look smaller.

I can never find the right size purse. The purse needs compartments. One slot for the box of TicTacs, another slot for the Orbit pack of gum, and how about a pocket for the cell phone? All of these items are the same size. I have been in church when my phone rang! I hastily reached in, shuffled things around, and grabbed what I thought was the phone. It was the TicTacs. Always refreshing but not at this particular moment.

Another tip. Don't step up to the cashier with a big, fat purse and try to find your wallet by shoving the contents to the left and right. I know you have seen these clowns. For a minute or longer, the purse gets jiggled left, right and bounced around. The explanation given for the delay: "My wallet is usually right here in the side compartment." Then to find the elusive wallet, this obnoxious individual starts removing the contents of the purse, and placing them on the counter. Hello? Was that a can of pork and beans that she just took out of her bag?

PERFUME

You may find the guy who prefers the scent of bacon dabbed behind your ears. *Lucky you!* But perfume can be a big ticket item. Designer perfume costs more than a condo in Cleveland so choose carefully.

Actresses go on *Letterman,* and he will compliment them on their perfume! Well, I want to smell that good too but these actresses won't reveal anything. Selfish. I want to hear exactly what the fragrance is. Where it was purchased. Give it up! Then, I wonder if they bought it at the 99 Cents Only Store and are embarrassed to admit it.

Finding a fragrance is challenging. After three good sniffs of the samples, your nose needs to rest. Try to evaluate your own essence. Avoid that strong stuff that can make paint peel. *Always, always* test a perfume for a day because each person's body chemistry changes the fragrance. You can try on something in the store that is heavenly. Two hours later, the fragrance has evolved into a smell that is similar to cow sweat.

MAKE YOUR BUTT LOOK SMALLER!

Oprah is featuring how to make your butt look smaller. I'm going to watch and record it at the same time. I don't want to miss anything! Something this important should be covered by *Anderson Cooper's 360°* on CNN. Actually, it's easy to make your butt look smaller. Walk into the room and then back out of the room when you leave. No one will ever see your butt. What is the hysteria all about? *Tricky but it can be done.*

A technique to slim down one's butt is being promoted by a company on the internet. They are offering some shorts with special water-proof pockets on the back. The pockets are used for little cool packs to trim down your butt. Place the packs in the freezer. After the packs are nice and cold, they go into the pockets of the shorts. Somehow the interaction of the cold against your white fat cells can reduce them or make them go away completely!

I can't afford those shorts. They're about a hundred dollars. I made my own. I took an old pair of jeans and safety-pinned some Ziploc bags inside the butt area. I filled the bags with ice cubes. I look pretty silly, and it's uncomfortable to sit down. But a little suffering is to be expected if you can get rid of the white fat cells with just the ice cubes from your refrigerator.

SHOES

Don't overlook what he has on his feet! *Decent shoes?* If his feet are exposed, are his toes clean? Nails polished? Are his shoes fashionable or walkable? How about simple and sensible? Does he wear socks with shower flip-flops? Maybe he works in an office so he wears those slip-ons with tassels. Are his shoes crafted of leather or painted-over cardboard?

We never needed to be as concerned about shoes as now. *Why now?* Because you need to refinance your house to buy a pair. Fashionable, wearable, walkable. Do designers of footwear know that we put these things on our feet? We then have to walk in them.

Years ago, I could afford to buy a couple pairs of shoes at one time. Fun colors. Simple flats. Now the simple flat doesn't exist anymore. It is $650! How difficult is it to make a shoe? Couches sell for less! At least you can sit on a couch!

Recently, a report came out about women, high heels and orgasms. YES, you read that correctly. Italy has reported that wearing high heels means good sex. Walking in high heels strengthens the pelvis. Now I regret more than ever that I cannot wear high heels. When I do try to wear them, I wobble and am visibly in excruciating pain. I feel left out of the party.

What's the biggest insult when it comes to being able to look good and walk that sexy walk in the highest of high heels? It's when a cross dresser can wear an outrageous outfit, put on the stilettos, stroll along casually and look sexier than me on my best day.

TATTOOS

The tattoo. It's the "in thing." Do you have one, two or thirty? I have none. The whole idea scares me. But everyone is getting them. Frankly, I don't get it. More than likely you'll be meeting up with a guy who has one or he may have a hundred. Who knows these days? Overindulgence is found at the tattoo parlors. I guess once you start, you can't stop. *I wouldn't know.* I couldn't so much as have them tattoo a *dot* on my skin, let alone a 10-inch Madonna and Child!

You may admire someone for going through the pain of getting a tattoo. Or think they're stupid. For any display of inkage, I do believe they must have a strong emotional or compelling reason as to why they chose to have needles stuck into their skin over and over again. This is a heavy psychological issue.

Plenty of empty-headed yahoos can be tattooed with "*I love big boobs.*" It's the rare ones who get something insightful. *"He who does not hope to win has already lost."* At least the guy who has this tattoo has more than 11 brain cells functioning.

For the person who wants the display of ink but is reluctant to undergo the permanent application, Chanel sells temporary tattoos. The collection includes lace, birds, flowers, leaves and chains for placement anywhere on your body. Those media types covering the runways and the red carpets have described them as simply gorgeous and a stunning fashion statement. The prediction is that the temporary tattoos will become the ultimate accessory for casual or formal occasions. I haven't seen Diane Sawyer with one yet but she may not be able to resist a little bird on her forehead. I keep tuning in so I won't miss the fun.

During my daughter's My Little Pony phase I walked around wearing stickers and tattoos all of the time. My arm had a herd of pink and purple ponies for days at a time. Barbie soon followed as did Hello Kitty and friends. My face would occasionally be adorned with one or all of them as well.

I was taking Christina to pre-school one morning when she said I needed two stickers to help me through the day. She carefully applied them to my cheeks. After dropping her off, I went to a client meeting. As I was being introduced to the staff, I looked in the conference room mirror. There like two big headlights were hot pink Barbie stickers on both cheeks! I casually explained to all of the executives that they were gifts from my four-year-old daughter.

I left the stickers right where they were and proceeded to give my presentation.

ETIQUETTE AND TABLE MANNERS

Picture a lovely little bistro. You and he are there for a quiet dinner. I happen to be sitting at another table with my boyfriend. I watch as your salad is served. You begin to eat. He begins to eat. With mouths wide open, you are both chewing your food and showing it to everyone else. What sits before me is the collapse of Western Civilization. This is not acceptable. If you can tolerate a man sitting across from you chewing with his mouth wide open, then you and he should be at home eating from Styrofoam containers. I have had meals completely ruined by people who evidently were raised by hyenas. *Learn how to eat.* Watch *Rachel Ray*. Then come out in public again.

I use my napkin like a bib. My dinner partners sometimes laugh at me. *Why?* I would rather not use my blouse to provide the evidence of what I ate at my last meal. Another issue is how to protect yourself when you snack. A chip with guacamole is a complete hazard. Swedish meatballs in sauce are a curse. You go to a party and can destroy a beautiful outfit by indulging in Pizza Pockets. Hosts should issue those disposable bibs for the purpose of protecting guests from the errant greasy crumb, sauce glob, and pasta splot. Designer bibs from Michael Kors would be smashing!

JUST BE YOURSELF!

Who or what are you? *Do you know?* It would be excellent to have some idiosyncrasies to make you more interesting and intriguing. I have ringing in my ears. My hearing is compromised because of it. But on the plus side, when someone talks to me, my "disability" adds a sweet "Bells from St. Mary's" accompaniment to their voice.

Singing in the car could be considered an idiosyncrasy. Be careful though about any choreography which takes your hands off of the steering wheel. Driving the car, and doing the arm motions to "YMCA" could have you free falling off a bridge before you get to the "A." Singing is so liberating … it's like therapy! If the guy you are dating can sing harmony with you, that is the best of all worlds! I believe therapists should recommend singing in the car to their patients.

Rich and I always sing in the car together. One of our favorite songs is "Get the Party Started" by Pink. It requires, what I call, honest enthusiasm for your vocals. The next level after the honest enthusiasm is getting to scream in a song.

The Who's Roger Daltrey is the luckiest person in the world. He gets to scream in a lot of their songs. I always join in with him when I am in my car. It feels wonderful! Don't tell me that you don't carry on this way when you're in the car. *How dull is your life?*

I sincerely believe that most convicted criminals did not sing in their cars. Maybe their lives of crime could have been avoided. They could have gotten completely absorbed in the effort of singing and striving for harmonies like the Osmonds. Plus, when you're in that group mentality, you're always trying to one-up the other person. That means they could have spent hours in the car perfecting their singing skills. Maybe they would have enjoyed being in the car so much that they wouldn't have gotten out of it to rob a liquor store. If I'm lucky, I'll get a grant for $200,000 to research my theory.

*S*EXY, SEX APPEAL

PHEROMONES

Pheromones. They're produced by men and women. It's a chemical that attracts the opposite sex, makes you desirable, and impacts your love life. To bring it down to the most basic level, it's when you say, "That guy is so hot." He has got it and it is filling the room! Sex appeal gone wild. That is how pheromones work. *Kind of. Sort of.*

Do you think you have enough? Maybe you need more. It would be nice if we could run into the mall and pick some up. The Internet is chock-full of information about pheromones and potions to be purchased. *Get out that credit card now!* Some vendors limit how much you can buy at one time! They don't want to be liable when their product transforms you into a hot, sexy man magnet. Your life will spin out of control! Too many men and too little time!

I am calling for a two-month supply.

A warning about being LOUD while having sex. In the United Kingdom, a couple was cited for being too noisy! The couple's screams during sex frightened neighbors and, even worse, drowned out the neighbor's television. The neighbors demanded the officials measure the "noise." The police concluded the "noise" ranged between 30 to 47 decibels. Loud but certainly not on par with the roar of a jet engine which is what one neighbor claimed.

As the officers filled out the report, they had to hold back their laughter when the neighbors stated, for the record, how furious they were about the frequency that the couple made love. They were shaking with anger when they remarked, "We are being subjected to this "noise" day in and day out!"

One elderly gentlemen commented, "This couple seems to be having sex all of the time!"

Which brings me to an interesting survey of men in their 70s. When asked what they regretted not doing more of, they responded, "If I had it to do all over again, I would have had more sex."

COUGARS

Cougars are here to stay. Get used to attractive older women or wealthy older women dating younger men. *So what?* Men have done this for years. These are women who are dating younger men because they want to and they can. *So, shut up.*

THE MISCELLANEOUS STUFF

YOU ARE WHAT YOU DRIVE

In Los Angeles, this car stuff is a curse. *"You are what you drive."* You're judged by your ownership of a Porsche, a Mini-Van or a Rolls Royce. We all do what we can to get what reflects our taste but it's our budget that dictates what we end up driving. Yeah, well, if your Prince Charming drives a dirty Yugo, he better look like George Clooney to make up for this lapse in judgment. Always keep in mind that any car can be leased or rented for a day to impress people.

Also, this is your (you know who you are) official notice to clean up your act! Stuffed animals in the back window of your car *do not* make you look attractive. Who started this nonsense? Plush critters from zebras to cats, dogs, lions, turtles, cows all lined up, standing side-by-side staring out the back window … *at me.* Twenty, 30 or 50 is a conservative estimate!

They're merely a mound of fading, dusty animals, and I don't care if you named them all. *They look stupid. They look tacky.* If this is a new trend, I'm not reading about it on any blogs. However if any *one* person would find it to be a delightful novelty, it could be Lady Gaga.

Furthermore, I have never had anyone ask me, "How many stuffed animals do *you* drive around with?" There are no children in the cars I have seen because, if that were the case, the animals would have been tossed haphazardly into the back window like TOYS. No, these stuffed animals are *positioned* in the back window staring at me while I wait in traffic behind them.

At times, I've seen such an incredible mound that there was the threat of the window being blocked completely. That is an automobile accident waiting to happen and a future case for *People's Court!*

If you or someone you know is guilty of this aberration, please set the critters free by giving them to some sweet deserving children. However, after being in the back window too long, the animals get faded and dirty and should be thrown into the trash … having served no good purpose while on this earth.

Moving on to another important subject … *cars and directions.* It's said that men don't like taking directions or referring to maps. I wonder about GPS units. Are men believing their manhood is threatened by this technology? Or do they feel that they're in control when they demand the shortest route anywhere — even if it happens to be a fire road across a mountain range?

Urgent warning about GPS. If you decide to take a trip through the United States, be careful about taking the shortest route from here to there. These little diversions can be dangerous. They may not be intended for passenger vehicles. Some examples …

In Florida, they have special roads through the Everglades for swamp boats and tracker vehicles. It's imperative that you double check your GPS if you're looking for the shortest routes when you're down there. Price of admission here would be water moccasins slithering up your pant legs if you drive your car into so much as one foot of water. Not too long ago, they discovered an anaconda (another huge South American snake who asphyxiates its prey) moving gracefully through a swamp. Yep, a large snake is something you want sliding into your wheel well and into the engine compartment! This is reason enough to stay away from Florida! What is worse: *the huge snake, alligator or the humidity?* You know, if it's too humid, you can suffocate in your sleep. *Honest. I think so, anyway.*

Out in the Iowa farmlands, your GPS could guide you through the middle of a corn field when in actuality the road is intended for tractor access. That shortcut would be a pretty drive but *bumpy.* Plus, you may miss some important tourist attractions along that main highway. In a moment, I will use a road trip through Arkansas to illustrate.

I prefer getting maps and a booklet from the Automobile Club. I trust them to guide me. They are more fun than the GPS because the Auto Club will mention places you should stop and visit. Like when you're traveling along Arkansas Highway 167 — how can anyone not want to spend an hour in Bald Knob, Arkansas, at Aunt Dot's Possum on a Stick, Fried Chicken and Gift Emporium?

One final comment about GPS. I want to have a choice when it comes to which "voice" is giving me directions. With today's technology, they will soon allow us to download different voices. I would be delighted to drive around listening to Brian or Stewie from *Family Guy.* Hugh Jackman wouldn't be bad either.

TECHNOLOGY

Yes, here again, 10 seconds from now everything I have written below will be obsolete!

Is he using the newest phone? *Are you?* Bluetooth, BlackBerry, stereo, text messaging, iPhone, music playback, video, or does he have a Jitterbug? People are quite impressed when you have all of this technology and know how to use it. I do not.

When going out to dinner, please don't have the cell phones at the table. I have watched couples on a date spending more time reading their text messages than talking with each other. Their phones are sitting just above their plates at an angle so anything incoming can be spotted. Are these people surgeons on call or advising the President of the United States? Why can't they enjoy a dinner without this interference?

Texting, at least, is a quiet activity. That is, unless you have a dopey alarm going off to let you (and the world around you) know that there's a new message. When you text, you can communicate 24/7 but have a code for the end of the exchange. Text messages are often statements. Nobody says, "Bye." That's why it's tricky to know when someone has finished the conversation. You can have friends and loved ones sitting and staring at their phones for days waiting for you to reply.

Additionally, don't text while you're driving a car unless you want a telephone pole in the middle of your forehead.

I refuse to walk with anyone, male or female, when they have a Bluetooth in their ear, and they don't warn me when they're taking a call. Plenty of times, I have carried on a conversation with someone not realizing that they weren't talking to me at all! *Yeah, don't you feel stupid?*

What about when someone is walking toward you, talking, smiling, and you respond with a greeting even though they're a stranger? The rule here is if you're the one with the plug in the ear and conversing with someone on the phone; *do not* make eye contact with anyone. See, if you look at me while you're talking, I automatically think you're addressing *me*. Whether you're a stranger or not, it doesn't matter. I am polite. I will greet you and smile. That's when I see you look away, off into the distance. You weren't talking to me *at all*. You are on one of those phones that can hardly be seen. Then I feel like a dope. Now, that's just plain sad.

I *do* have a cell phone. I call people, and people call me. *Pretty simple.* However, I admit that I often misplace my cell phone around the house and in the car. I then have to call it to locate it. I chase around listening for the ringing phone. When I finally locate it, a message is displayed ("Missed Call") and I wonder who it was.

Recently, I heard the most shocking news story having to do with a cell phone and a gun! The driver of a SUV was on his way home when his new, hands-free cell phone rang. It startled him to such an extent that he veered off the road, went through a guardrail, and plunged into a river! The vehicle was filling with water, and he couldn't escape through the door or the window. He was getting desperate! He had to think fast. He reached up to his Easy Rider Rifle Rack, grabbed a gun, shot the windshield out of his SUV and swam to the surface.

I've seen those helpful shows when they demonstrate what to do in an emergency like this. The vehicle falls into a lake. First, stay calm. That's as far as I would get with the instructions if this disaster would befall me! Three seconds later, I would be drowning. The idea is to stay calm and use a little metal hammer-like device to break the window. Never have I seen them encourage the viewers to arm themselves with a gun to shoot their way out of the car.

I know my confidence level would be higher if I didn't have to punch through the window. Will I be able to see where the window is? I have bad eyesight so if I am underwater, my contact lenses would float away. But being prepared is what counts. You can't control the circumstances, just how you react to them. Finding the little hammer in my purse is the challenge! While I am sinking into the abyss, I would be digging around in my purse for it. Do you really think I could find it amongst the lipsticks, gum and Snickers bars? I would be a goner.

YOUR TYPE

You, in your heart and head, probably know what your type is. Friends and family members may not have a clue but they still try to direct your attention to someone who is single, otherwise available, or desperate for a date. That these friends or family members aren't more discriminating is a puzzle to me.

173

In the situation that follows, it shows that my brother had nothing but absolute contempt for me when he decided to introduce me to his neighbor. He argued later that *contempt* was not the appropriate description. He just likes a good joke and, as my older brother, he should be given *carte blanche!* He'll always be my older brother so this nonsense will never end!

When you have the opportunity to visit out-of-town family or friends, chances are that there is someone of the opposite sex that you absolutely must meet. It could be rewarding, interesting or another one of those nightmarish close encounters. Believe me, the stars were aligned when I went to visit my brother Bert in the wilds of Northern Nevada. Bert, who has a wicked sense of humor, told me that his next door neighbor was a handsome, happy-go-lucky bachelor who brags about being a chick magnet. OK, I was curious.

My brother added, "You really need to meet this guy. You never can tell. This could be the one!"

Right. This evaluation was coming from my brother who thinks a good time is a 3 a.m. wake-up call to go ice fishing in below-freezing weather. *I was skeptical.* We walked over to the neighbor's house in the early evening. When we arrived at the front door, my brother introduced us. Dave's beard and tattoos didn't intimidate me but his booming voice was two decibels above a turbine engine. Friendly but LOUD! Bert suggested

Dave give me a tour of the house, and I should walk back to my brother's place later.

Dave guided me into the front hall and directed my attention to the spacious living room. Every wall was brick-red with a single mirrored one over on the far side. I figured that he must have removed a dining room and a spare bedroom to allow for the expansion of this living room. He motioned over to the black slate bar that proudly displayed a large jar of Slim Jims. Dave mentioned that he served those as appetizers when he had guests over. *Yummy.* The wall was illuminated with several neon signs featuring the liquor he served. If I wanted a Bud Light, Coors, Heineken, Dos Equis or Tecate, I was good to go.

Over to the side was a video game setup, a custom-made pool table, and large hi-def TV, and in the far corner sat another smaller bar with a beer tap which served a Samuel Adams beverage. Obviously, this was Beer Drinker's Heaven.

Near the beer area and adjacent to the shelves with the hard liquor were his guns. Twelve or fifteen were displayed behind glass. I was just hoping a firearm demonstration wouldn't be part of the tour. Luckily, there was so much more to see so we continued on to a back sun-porch. There, he announced, was his latest addition — a large, six person hot tub. A special sunroof had been installed as well so he and his guests could see the stars while relaxing in the hot tub. Dave mentioned how everything was remotely controlled and absolutely state-of-the-art.

He added, "The ladies never have any complaints." *I betcha!*

This is where I need to explain a wee bit more about him. He has a trophy collection which is proudly displayed throughout this rambling, ranch-style home. No bowling trophies, mind you. Dave is an avid hunter. He kills it. He guts it. He stuffs it. He eats it. With as many animals as were displayed, his freezers could supply him sustenance for at least 50 years! Every room, every ledge, in every corner, next to anyplace you would stand or sit is a taxidermy animal of some type. They all stared at me. It was like a natural history museum. Completely, forever dead deer, antelope, pheasant, coyote, duck, fox, cougar, boar, bear, armadillo. I haven't listed all of them either! I was surprised that there wasn't a stuffed canary in the bunch! Then to think the last thing each one of these poor creatures saw was this yahoo with a gun in his hand!

This was a little more than my sensibilities could take. I thanked him for his tour, turned down the offer of a beer, and dashed back over to my brother's house. As I bolted through the front door, my brother began laughing hysterically. "You mean you didn't stay for some of his hospitality? Wasn't he *your type?*"

Exactly what frame of reference was my brother using?

ASTROLOGY

When you're introduced to a potential date, do you ask, "What sign are you?"

I'm not deep into astrological signs and horoscopes. I have more of a passing interest. For example, I would like to know if Aquarius would be more compatible with me than Leo. But if the Leo was really good looking and had a lot of money, I could overlook the fact that we weren't compatible. Others want to know if you're a *true* Leo or a *true* Aries. I have no idea how one fits into this concept of *true.*

I am a Sagittarian. According to astrology.com, my inner self is passionate about big-game fishing. *Did I read that right?* Sure, I love to eat tuna but I rely on StarKist to get it for me. *Does that count?*

There are men who are guided by the stars. It could be an interesting dynamic in your relationship. Then again, it could drive you cuckoo! I have no good advice for this kind of a situation. Astrology is very similar to politics. Some people are ferociously serious about it. Is Jupiter in the sign of Pisces, and where is Saturn going to be next Tuesday? At the Bruce Springsteen concert? *How would I know?*

Daily horoscopes are interesting to read. But they are very nonspecific: "You will travel somewhere today." Wow, that's right! I *am* going to the grocery store.

My advice is to be cautious about the astrologically-minded. Respect them if they are firm believers. They are sincere.

I had my chart done years ago. It was pages and pages of details. Far too much to bother reading. Maybe I should have paid more attention to it! There could have been indicators directing me to my real life's calling–a brain surgeon, heavy equipment operator, President of the United States.

PARKING ETIQUETTE

Easy. Always valet park. Tip.

$\mathcal{M}$AGIC HAPPENS

LOVE AT FIRST SIGHT

You can tell me something and overnight I will forget it. I'll try to remember what you said but usually my brain cells will shove it out of the way. Details like which litigant won on *Judge Judy* take precedence. But when it came to my first encounter with love at first sight, I can remember the entire experience like it was an hour ago. *It was exciting!* His face burned into my corneas like laser surgery. It's a visual that never goes away. Prepare yourself for it because love at first sight is not for the faint of heart!

Picture a beautiful summer day in a leafy, quiet suburb in the Los Angeles area. I am 17. I returned from the beach and I had parked my car in the driveway. I was taking out the towels, air mattresses and food when I heard the low rumble of a car cruising down the street. The muffler was making the statement to me, "Hot car coming. Hot guy coming." *Sure enough, I wasn't disappointed.*

It was a rusty-red primer 1956 Chevy, clearly in the stages of becoming a muscle car. I needed to get him to stop. *Why? I don't know!* I think I had way too much sun that day at the beach because this behavior was bordering on sun stroke! *Should I pretend to be hitchhiking to get him to stop? How about a free car wash?* There was no time to make a sign. What was wrong with me? *I was smitten.*

The car was now close enough for me to make out chrome rims on the wheels. While the car had announced itself with that hot-rod muffler sound, it wasn't obnoxious. I imagined the driver of the car was pretty much the same — wanting to be noticed but low key, classy. I was completely captivated; I stared as the car came closer and closer.

Then, suddenly, there is a "boom" — like a loud popping noise. The hood from the engine compartment shot up into the air. The hood detached from its hinges and took flight … 20 feet up! It sailed over the car doing a somersault and landed with a loud clank and thud behind the car on the pavement. *Wow! What a stunt!*

The car quickly pulled up to the curb. I studied the driver as he emerged. *Be still my heart.* For a moment, I think I stopped breathing! I heard birds singing! I was getting light-headed! He was tall, wore Levi's, white t-shirt, had dark brown/black hair. He walked over to the hood, lifted it up and placed it in the yard in front of my house. He looked over at me but said nothing.

I excused his unfriendly behavior, figuring he was in shock.

Granted, this was an odd accident/incident — whatever you want to call it. I considered it my lucky day! Lucky for him too because I was on hand to offer my assistance. Was he traumatized? Perhaps he could use a refreshing beverage?

I approached him, smiled and said, "Hi!"

He just nodded. He was at least 6'2" and thin. Spectacular blue eyes and great lashes! He had beautiful skin with a little bit of that beard stubble. *How very lovely. How very gorgeous!* I think I stopped breathing again! By now, I didn't know my own name. His lips were perfection.

I was pretty much rendered speechless. *Well, almost.* I asked in my most demure way, *"Can I help you?"* Yeah, like I was going to lift the hood back onto the car and bolt it down! He wasn't much for conversation, only asking if he could leave the hood right there in the yard until he could retrieve it later that evening. We agreed on a time, and we left it at that.

A few minutes later, I wondered if I'd been hallucinating! Did he tell me his name? Where does he live? What if he never returned to get the crumpled car hood? This had the potential to turn into a disaster of epic proportions! Yet, to me, he was Prince Charming.

No white horse, but a high performance Chevy would do. *I'm not picky.* I went through my potential boyfriend checklist. Yes, this was love at first sight.

I positioned myself in the front yard. I was not going to miss his return. I refused bathroom breaks, dinner, phone calls because this was a life-changing experience. You can only imagine how I felt when I finally heard that rumble coming down the street and saw that car pull up to the curb. He got out and walked up to me. With a magnificent smile, he said, "Well, here I am again. By the way, my name is Mike."

Mr. Love at First Sight became Husband #1.

ⵄDDS OF GETTING MARRIED REVISITED

That statistic I mentioned at the beginning of this book is a bunch of nonsense — *a woman over age 40 has a better chance of being killed by a terrorist than of getting married.* In fact, it has often been questioned, and many now say the research was flawed. The way the press presented the statistic allowed readers to jump to conclusions. Who was to blame for that? Did they intend to cause panic throughout the nation? In fact, the immediate reaction bordered on hysteria!

Today, you can go online and check what your chances are of getting married. Answer a few questions, enter your age, and the calculator will give you the odds. As a side note, this website adds, "Having a lot of money can increase your odds exponentially!" (www.calculatorslive.com)

It's not that there are fewer men in the world. By 2020, more than 24 million Chinese men of marrying age could find themselves without a woman to wed. I'm wondering if I should learn their language and head on over? Does that mean 24 million men to one woman? That statistic can make you positively giddy!

The ratios we have to rely on for the United States come from our national census. If you want the odds of 171 men to 100 women, go to Cusseta, GA or Chattahoochee County, GA. How about Union County, Florida (179 men to 100 women); or Crowley County, Colorado (200 men to 100 women). Actually, I'm suspicious. In Crowley County, there is a correctional facility. To come up with the ratio, did they include the men who are incarcerated?

I don't know if traveling to far off lands will make the difference in finding Prince Charming. *It could!* I see it as an invitation to a new way of living … unconventional, outrageous, unusual, uninhibited and imaginative!

A few years ago, census data was published by Singleton, New South Wales, Australia. They counted 201 men to every 100 women. These men have lovely accents! *Yummy!* Those are, indeed, impressive numbers — again, that was *201 men to 100 women!* The town has adopted its own signature song originally performed by the Weather Girls! *"It's raining men. Hallelujah!"*

Bye for now. I'm on my way to the airport. I'm going to Singleton! Of course, if that doesn't work out, there's always China!